WEEKDAY WARRIOR

Margaret White

Published by Warner House Press of Albertville, Alabama USA

Copyright © 2022 Margaret White
Cover Design © 2022 Ablaze Media
Interior Design © 2022 Warner House Press

All rights reserved. No part of this book may be used or reproduced in any manner whatsoever without written permission, except in the case of brief quotations in critical articles and reviews. For more information, contact

Warner House Press
1325 Lane Switch Road
Albertville, Alabama 35951
USA

Published 2022
Printed in the United States of America

Apple image by rawpixel.com

Unless otherwise noted, all scripture quotations are taken fromthe New American Standard Bible® (), Copyright © 1960, 1962, 1963, 1968, 1971, 1972, 1973, 1975, 1977, 1995 by The Lockman Foundation Used by permission.

Scripture quotations marked AMPC taken from the Amplified® Bible, Copyright © 1954, 1958, 1962, 1964, 1965, 1987 by The Lockman Foundation Used by permission. www.lockman.org

Scripture quotations marked ESV are from The Holy Bible, English Standard Version®, Copyright © 2001 by Crossway Bibles, a publishing ministry of Good News Publishers. Used by permission. All rights reserved.

Scripture quotations marked KJV are from The Authorized (King James) Version. Rights in the Authorized Version in the United Kingdom are vested in the Crown. Reproduced by permission of the Crown's patentee, Cambridge University Press.

Scripture quotations marked NIV are taken from HOLY BIBLE, NEW INTERNATIONAL VERSION®. Copyright © 1973, 1978, 1984 by International Bible Society. Used by permission of Zondervan Publishing House.

Scripture quotations marked NKJV are from the New King James Version®. Copyright © 1982 by Thomas Nelson. Used by permission. All rights reserved.

Scripture quotations marked NLT are from the Holy Bible, New Living Translation, Copyright © 1996, 2004, 2007, 2013, 2015 by Tyndale House Foundation. Used by permission of Tyndale House Publishers Inc., Carol Stream, Illinois 60188. All rights reserved.

26 25 24 23 22 1 2 3 4 5

ISBN: 978-1-951890-42-1

I want to thank all of you who serve Jesus through the gift of teaching. Thank you for pouring your life into His children. Thank you for the time on your knees, the tears, and the sleepless nights balanced by the hugs and laughter. Thank you for always working to be better. Thank you for staying when so many are leaving. You are part of the fivefold ministry. What would we do without you? Stand firm Weekday Warriors.

Many thanks to Rachelle Hodge who not only made me a better teacher but suggested that I write this book. Thank you for your encouragement and instruction. I'm forever grateful.

Thank you to my friends and church family. You are precious to me.

I dedicate this book to my exceptionally wonderful family. To my husband, Harold, who always supported me in my dreams. To my children, Michelle and Allen, Nathan and Candi, Betsy and Brandon, and Sarah and Jacob, for their faithful encouragement. And to my wonderful grandchildren, who are my delight. Ashley, Hannah, Andrew, Miciah, Cameron, Caleb, Noelle, Chloe, Addison, David, Thomas, Amelia, Rhett, Houston, McCoy, and Alyssa.

Contents

Week 1	1		Week 20	115
Week 2	7		Week 21	121
Week 3	13		Week 22	127
Week 4	19		Week 23	133
Week 5	25		Week 24	139
Week 6	31		Week 25	145
Week 7	37		Week 26	151
Week 8	43		Week 27	157
Week 9	49		Week 28	163
Week 10	55		Week 29	169
Week 11	61		Week 30	175
Week 12	67		Week 31	181
Week 13	73		Week 32	187
Week 14	79		Week 33	193
Week 15	85		Week 34	199
Week 16	91		Week 35	205
Week 17	97		Week 36	211
Week 18	103			
Week 19	109			

Week 1

Week 1 Day 1: Days of Preparation

"THE EARTH WAS WITHOUT FORM AND VOID, AND DARKNESS WAS OVER THE FACE OF THE DEEP. AND THE SPIRIT OF GOD WAS HOVERING OVER THE FACE OF THE WATERS." GENESIS 1:2 ESV

A new school year begins. You've been working in your classroom for weeks, preparing. Hovering. The Hebrew word translated as hover means to brood, flutter, move, and shake. Brood means to think deeply about or hatch something. That is a good description of what you're doing.

Every good beginning requires some hovering. Imagine the Holy Spirit hovering over formless earth, thinking deeply, hatching plans. Similarly, you hover over your room to make the most of your space. You think deeply about your plans and establishing your procedures the first day. You move and shake putting up your room décor. You anguish over seating arrangements. You are hatching a new school year. It's a huge task, but you set about it with vigor because that's what you do. You bring form, fullness, and light to the deep unknown of the school year. Before you know it, you'll be hovering over the faces of those God-chosen little hatchlings you will spend the next nine months brooding over.

While you hover over your school year, the Spirit of God hovers over you. He fills you with the knowledge of His will; He enables you to do all things; He refreshes and renews and restores; He gives you the mind of Christ. Yes, He hovers over you.

"FOR I KNOW THE PLANS I HAVE FOR YOU, DECLARES THE LORD. THEY ARE PLANS FOR GOOD AND NOT FOR EVIL, TO GIVE YOU A FUTURE AND A HOPE." JEREMIAH 29:11 TLB

Does that sound familiar? It sounds like the same plans you are hatching for your students. Plans for good, not evil, plans for their future and to give them hope?

 # Week 1 Day 2: The Beginning

"And God said, "Let there be light," and there was light."
Genesis 1:3 ESV

It's the beginning of school. Yesterday you spent the day establishing procedures and getting to know your students. You created light. Light brings order out of darkness and chaos. That's what you did. All day long you were bringing light to every corner of your room.

When the Lord hovered over the beginning of His creation, the first thing He decided to do was bring light onto the scene—illumination, clarity. In Hebrew, the word translated "light" even indicates happiness. Your classroom management and procedures are the light of your classroom. It's the first thing you must establish in the beginning.

When God said, "Let there be light," He settled for nothing less than light. Light was His goal and that's what He produced.

When God created light He wasn't wishy-washy. If He said, "Let there be light," and only dimness occurred, would He accept that? Would He say, "Oh, that's close enough?" No, nothing less than light would do. You must have the same determination as you establish the light in your classroom. God was determined but He was also gracious. It's a tricky combination but you have it because you have Him inside you. You establish your procedures and you don't back off. You let your love and good humor shine through in the establishing of it. Of course you are anxious to get on to Spelling List 1, but at this point in the beginning it's most crucial to "Let there be light."

Week 1 Day 3:
Bridge Over Troubled Waters

"And God said, "Let there be an expanse between the waters to separate water from water." Genesis 1:6 NIV

You are beginning to develop a relationship with your students. This is a tricky thing. You want to blend but you also have to be separate. You walk the room, get down to their level, laugh and cry with them, but you must also hold yourself apart. Be careful in these early days to establish that expanse between the waters. It IS possible to smile before Christmas!

God was very kind to Adam in the beginning. He made a beautiful garden for him, just like you made an engaging classroom. He gave Adam pets and a helper. He showed His love in many ways, yet God set Himself up as the authority. Loving but separate. He wasn't wishy-washy about His love or His rules.

By now, some of your "waters" are beginning to test your rules. The newness of the year is already wearing off and some will see how far they can push you. You must remain steady, professional and kind. You are the expanse, the bridge between your little waters and the growth that needs to be accomplished this year.

"You are the light of the world. A city set on a hill cannot be hidden." Matthew 5:14 ESV

You are not the waters, you are the light, you are the city on the hill, you are the authority. When God separated the waters and created the expanse, the Bible says, "And it was so." The word *so* means it was set right. Even though you might be weary of procedure and practice, you are setting things right. You establish yourself as the bridge and your little waters learn to flow under you, under your authority.

Love your students, smile at them, laugh with them, but remember to be the expanse, not the waters.

Week 1 Day 4:
It was Good

"God saw all that he had made, and it was very good."
Genesis 1:31 NIV

By now you are beginning to know the character of your students. And I'm sure you have some characters! Let's talk about God's character a little today. He is good. When bad things happen, He is still good. It's what He IS.

Psalm 136:1 says, "Give thanks to the Lord, for He is good." Part of God's identity is that He is good.

My mom was always trying to find the perfect but easy fudge recipe. Sometimes her fudge would be runny and sometimes hard, but it always tasted good.

God is always good too. When you can't find a place to seat that talkative student, God is good. When your new idea flops—and the administrator walks in, God is good. Great days and hard days are ahead of you this year but in them all, God is good. Even when it seems He isn't hearing your prayer. For example, when someone knocks on your door you immediately respond. You begin to move toward the door. The person on the outside can't see you moving. He might think you are not answering, but you are. Just because you don't see an immediate answer to your prayer, doesn't mean God isn't responding.

There is no shadow of turning in God. He always responds and it's always good. When we walk with our good God, He works good in our lives and the lives of our kids. God is always moving toward good. His plans for your school year are good. He will provide you the keys to your kids, the inspiration that is beyond your creativity, and the love that your heart can't produce.

It will be very good, like fudge.

Week 1 Day 5: Not Good

"It is not good for the man to be alone; I will make him a helper suitable for him." Genesis 2:18

The first year I hatched chicks in my class, the lady who gave me the eggs told me to send the chicks in pairs to their new homes. She said they wouldn't survive alone.

It's also not good for man to be alone. Sure, it's easy to isolate yourself in your classroom. You have lessons to plan and papers to grade but your soul will shrink. When you live and breathe school, you're like an ostrich with his head stuck in the sand. You miss the refreshing breeze, the laughter, the life, the FUN! It's not good. Pull your head out of the sand, go down the hall, and pull someone else's head out of the sand. Make relationships with other teachers. You need each other.

A lie looms over your head saying you don't have time for relationships. You are depriving yourself of something vital to your survival. God knew Adam needed more than the animals in his classroom—I mean garden. He needed more than an evening walk with God. He needed a flesh and blood helpmate. So that's what God supplied.

"Confess your sins to each other and pray for each other so that you may be healed. The earnest prayer of a righteous person has great power and produces wonderful results." James 5:16 NLT

You need others and others need you. If planning and grading is eating all your free time, something's wrong. You will end up just another educational disaster. Adam needed more to life than plants and animals (plans and students). You need more out of life than school. Time to vent, times of refreshing, time with like-minded kindred spirits make you a better teacher. Teaching is draining. Let yourself be refilled.

"As iron sharpens iron, So a man sharpens the countenance of his friend." Proverbs 27: 17 NKJV

God intends for you to take turns lifting and building each other up. It's how the body of Christ works. It's part of the Jeremiah 29:11 plans: plans to prosper you and to give you hope and a future.

Week 2

Week 2 Day 1:
These Boots Were Made for Walking

"Every place on which the sole of your foot treads, I have given it to you." Joshua 1:3

It's week two. Many of you have already switched from your new cute shoes to your comfy old tennies. It will take a while to get used to standing all day again, but you'll get there.

If you haven't already, it's time to start doing a little classroom prayer walk first thing in the morning. It doesn't have to be long, Lord knows you don't have long. Walk through the room praising the Lord and inviting Him in. Ask Him to re-establish His order because it likely got lost along the way last week! Pass by each desk asking God to bless. If something comes to mind, pray it, but don't stress about praying a long powerful prayer for each one. Asking God to bless them isn't a cop out, it's powerful. As you ask Him to bless them you are bringing them up before the throne of God and seeking His best for them. That's pretty amazing!

Don't forget to pray for yourself on your morning prayer walk. Ask for freshness and anointing, for energy and creativity, and for the key to each child. Put on the full armor of God, clothe yourself in Christ, claim the mind of Christ and ears to hear what the Spirit of the Lord is saying.

A morning prayer walk in your room only takes a couple minutes. If you try it, you'll find it's supernatural. It's like tithing. When we first think about tithing, we think we don't have enough money to do it. We are already falling short each month, how can we possibly tithe? But when we try it, we are able to pay all the bills and have some left over. Supernatural. The budget of your school day will be more productive when you put on your comfy shoes and claim your territory for the Lord.

Week 2 Day 2:
Super Huper

"YET IN ALL THESE THINGS WE ARE MORE THAN CONQUERORS THROUGH HIM WHO LOVED US." ROMANS 8:37 NKJV

Joshua conquered Jericho like "more than a conqueror." He walked around it a bunch of times and the walls fell down. He stepped and the place was his. No bombs, no cannons, not even spears. The Greek word translated "more than a conqueror" is *hupernikao*. It means super-abundantly victorious. You are that kind of conqueror, a supernatural conqueror. You are in the realm of "immeasurably more than we can ask or imagine." How do I know? The Bible tells me so!

Our verse says, "in all these things" we are *hupernikao*. In what things? If we back up to Romans 8:35 we find the list of things. Tribulation, distress, persecution, famine, nakedness, peril, and sword. I don't mean to scare you but I'm afraid you will face most of these things this year. Like Dr. Seuss' Thing 1 and Thing 2, these "things" will try to wreak havoc in your class. The playground is full of tribulation, distress, and persecution. As for famine, there's always that one kid who forgets his lunch and is STARVING! Thank heavens for the dress code when nakedness issues arise. Peril? Here in Arizona we take 4th graders to the Grand Canyon. Talk about peril! And swords? Three little words: Show and Tell!

Don't be dismayed. You are more than a conqueror. You are super *hupernikao*! You aren't limited to mere earthly, natural means to deal with these "things." Like Joshua you have supernatural help. Remember in Joshua 5:13–14, Joshua is standing near Jericho and suddenly he sees a man with a drawn sword. The man says, "As commander of the army of the Lord I have now come." You have this same helper! You have the Holy Spirit dwelling in you. You have the Divine edge! There is nothing that can come along this year that you can't handle.

"SOME TRUST IN CHARIOTS AND SOME IN HORSES, BUT WE TRUST IN THE NAME OF THE LORD OUR GOD." PSALM 20:7 NIV

Week 2 Day 3: Ready Feet

"Great crowds came to him, bringing the lame, the blind, the crippled, the mute and many others, and laid them at his feet;" Matthew 15:30 NIV

Do you ever feel a little like Jesus must have felt? Great crowds surround you laying every imaginable problem "at your feet." They say teachers make over 10,000 decisions a day. And oh, the variety of decisions you make! "Is Chloe *really* sick?" "What can we do for the next twenty-five minutes since my thirty-minute activity only took five?" The lame, the blind, the crippled; oh, where are the mute? Decision after decision. But you handle it like a pro because that's what you are!

"With your feet fitted with the readiness that comes from the gospel of peace." Ephesians 6:15 NIV

As a teacher, your feet are always ready. Ready to run across the playground to tend a bloody nose, ready to fly to the restroom on a thirty second break! When you put on the shoes of peace your steps become supernatural.

Most of our armor is protective. Are our shoes of peace protection? The other day I was praying for a teacher friend who is in a very difficult situation. I heard myself praying for "Mighty Peace." I stopped for a second, thinking it sounded like an oxymoron. Can peace be mighty?

"For a child will be born to us.... And His name will be called Wonderful Counselor, Mighty God, Eternal Father, Prince of Peace." Isaiah 9:6

Two of the names of Jesus are Mighty God and Prince of Peace. So, I guess peace can be mighty! Your ready feet are shod in the good news of Mighty Peace. Like Joshua, every place you step, you are claiming. As you step with your mighty peace shoes, you confirm God's dominion in your room. All the things the great crowd lays at your feet come under the dominion of your Peace.

"You make him (us) to rule over the works of Your hands; You have put all things under his feet." Psalm 8:6

Ready feet, mighty peace.

Week 2 Day 4: Rainy Day Recess

"And rain fell on the earth." Genesis 7:12 NIV

Rainy day recess. The animals have been loaded onto the ark! All the craziness of recess contained under one roof. Suddenly you have a lot more sympathy for Noah.

Perhaps your plans for the day go right down the drain, with the rain. The copies you were going to make, that sip of caffeine you needed so badly, the moment to just breathe, gone. So, like the professional you are, you adjust your plans, pull up your big girl panties, and dig deep in your tool bag for an alternate plan.

"Consider it pure joy, my brothers, whenever you face trials of many kinds." James 1:2 NIV

Depending on your personality type and years of experience, rainy day recess can be nearly devastating. Remember, you are not alone in this. When Daniel was in the lion's den God sent His angel and shut the lions' mouths. (I wonder if that angel is available for classroom duty?) When Joseph was in the pit and in prison, the Lord was with him. When you encounter these interruptions to your carefully made plans, which is pretty often, you just need to turn to the wall for a quick prayer. Suddenly inspiration comes. A moment ago, you were a mindless zombie but now you can think clearly, and your thoughts are so creative! Why? Because the Creator of the heavens and the earth is your helper!

The problem is, we too often forget to stop and pray. We keep plowing along with our old plow.

"Jesus replied, 'No one who puts a hand to the plow and looks back is fit for service in the kingdom of God.'" Luke 9:62 NIV

You are not limited to your old familiar tools. Limitless resources are at hand when you stop and pray. Whether it's a rainy-day recess or a failed Kagan structure, if you pause and pray instead of trying to push through on your own strength, you will be amazed at the outcome.

Hand to the plow.

 # Week 2 Day 5: Stand Firm

Instead of early onset dementia, teachers sometimes suffer from early onset exhaustion. It's the first quarter and already you feel drained. You wonder if you can make it through the year. But, you can! Come on Eeyore, pin your tail back on. You can do this.

"STAND FIRM THEREFORE.... TAKING UP THE SHIELD OF FAITH WITH WHICH YOU WILL BE ABLE TO EXTINGUISH ALL THE FLAMING ARROWS OF THE EVIL ONE." EPHESIANS 6:14, 6:16

The naggy voice that says you won't make it is a liar, a flaming arrow of the evil one. It sneaks in to derail you when you're stressed, stretched, and weary. You think, "How can I be so tired this early in the year?" Easy. You're just getting to know your kiddos, discovering their strengths and weaknesses, and pondering how to help them—stretching. You're getting used to the routine of school, plus everything else in your life. Outside of the Christmas season, the beginning of the year requires the most energy. It doesn't mean you aren't able, it means you aren't used to it yet. Like any boot camp, it takes some getting used to. You are building stamina.

You need to lift up the shield of faith and quench those doubting thoughts. Resist lies and focus on the truth. This takes effort. What does God say? What does His Word say? *The calling of God is irrevocable. You are equipped and anointed.* In fact, you have a double portion anointing (2 Kings 2:9).

You do need to press into the Lord. You do need to carve out time to rest and refresh, like a recess. There are some who think recess is a waste of valuable teaching time. But in fact, more is accomplished when the kids have a break. You also need recess on a regular basis. You need a day or at least a half day when you don't do anything for school. If you don't allow yourself to refresh, you will burn out.

"YOU WERE TIRED OUT BY THE LENGTH OF YOUR ROAD, YET YOU DID NOT SAY, 'IT IS HOPELESS.' YOU FOUND RENEWED STRENGTH, THEREFORE YOU DID NOT FAINT." ISAIAH 57:10

Find that renewed strength.

Recess. Just do it.

Week 3

Week 3 Day 1: Reinforcements

"THEY ARE LIKE TREES PLANTED ALONG THE RIVERBANK, BEARING FRUIT EACH SEASON. THEIR LEAVES NEVER WITHER, AND THEY PROSPER IN ALL THEY DO." PSALM 1:3 NLT

You are like a tree planted by a river. In the high desert of Arizona this verse is very clear. You can always tell where water is because you'll see trees. In the desert, the river is their life.

"THEN THE ANGEL SHOWED ME A RIVER WITH THE WATER OF LIFE." REVELATION 22:1 NLT

You are a tree near the river. The river is God's Spirit and power. Your strength and life come from the river. Your students are like mistletoe. Mistletoe grows on the branches of the trees by the river. Mistletoe is a parasite. *Parasite* sounds bad; let's call it a symbiotic relationship. You benefit from the river and your students benefit from you. You grow and they grow. How? Because you are near the river.

In addition to planning and teaching and grading, you have the duty to maintain a vital relationship with your river—the Lord. As a Christian teacher you provide spiritual growth as well as academic growth. You must stay by the river. Your roots must go deep into the riverbed. If you drift away, your little *parasites*, I mean mistletoes, will suffer.

The students should see your relationship with the River all through the day. They shouldn't just hear about the Lord during Bible time. This takes purposeful intention. When they are struggling in Math, stop and pray. When they have writer's block, stop and pray. Let them see that you don't isolate time at the River to a Bible lesson. It will cause your mistletoes to grow.

"IN EVERY SITUATION, BY PRAYER AND PETITION, WITH THANKSGIVING, PRESENT YOUR REQUESTS TO GOD." PHILIPPIANS 4:6 NIV

In every situation be contagiously and consistently prayerful. Your mistletoe is counting on you.

Week 3 Day 2: Planted

"They are like trees planted along the riverbank." Psalm 1:3 NLT

Planted. I have a big old tree planted in my backyard. It's not here one day and gone the next. It's planted. God is too. He never leaves us or forsakes us. Not even on a Tuesday (in my opinion, the longest day of the week). Children need "planted" teachers. Life changes so quickly in many of their homes, often school and the teacher are the only stable factors.

The little guy in his second foster home or the kid who spends half the week with mom and half with dad. There is no way to change these situations, but you can provide some stability. You can be planted. Instead of being upset about the crazy circumstances which affect you as well as the child, you must show yourself to be planted on the kid's team. You are steady, smiling, forgiving, and understanding. Every day. Even when it's hard. You model love unconditionally because they need to see it. How can they understand God's great love if they never sample it?

"For God so loved the world that He gave His one and only Son." John 3:16 NIV

Can John 3:16 impact a child who's never experienced sacrificial love? You must be that planted tree. When they disrupt the class or fight you every inch of the way, when they are completely unlovable, you remain planted. Didn't God do that for you? They must see God's love in your eyes. You are the Esther in that child's life—for such a time as this.

You stand, planted. You love and listen when you want to run away. You smile when you want to cry. You hug the little body that needs a bath. Why? Because God made you the teacher, because God planted you in that life. That's what you do. And because you do, one child might just reach a little root out toward the River and be planted in Jesus.

Week 3 Day 3: Bearing Fruit

"They are like trees planted along the riverbank, bearing fruit each season." Psalm 1:3 NLT

Let's talk about bearing fruit. It's the beginning of the year and apparently everyone has forgotten all they learned in their previous years of school. You find yourself teaching and reteaching stuff they should already know. You have lots of new information they need to learn this year, lots of great plans, but you can't move forward until they get the old stuff.

"Sow your seed in the morning and do not be idle in the evening, for you do not know whether morning or evening sowing will succeed, or whether both of them alike will be good." Ecclesiastes 11:6

This is pretty much par for the course. Sure, they know that B says buh, or to round up if the number is 5 or over. They know you put a capital at the beginning of a sentence and there are three feet in a yard. This time of year they want to be seeds snuggled down in the soil, they don't want to stretch out their roots in new directions. It's not the fruit bearing season yet. There will be fruit, but first there must be planting, pruning, cultivating, weeding, and all the things necessary to produce good fruit. I grew up in farm country and if I remember right, the first step to bearing fruit is preparing the soil. Even though you're anxious to get on, if you try to grow a seed before the soil is ready, you won't bear a good crop.

"To everything there is a season." Ecclesiastes 3:1 NKJV

Don't stress. The Lord knows all you need to accomplish. Fruit will come. The Lord hovered over a void during creation. You can expect to do the same. You're facing the "darkness on the surface of the deep." Just hover a bit longer. There will be light. Seeds will grow. You will bear fruit. You are a tree planted by the River.

The River feeds you and you feed your seeds.

Week 3 Day 4: In the Groove

"HE LEADS ME BESIDE STILL WATERS. HE RESTORES MY SOUL."
PSALM 23:2-3 ESV

When surrounded by craziness and chaos it's a comfort to know God is leading us beside still waters. Still waters. The Hebrew word means a resting place, a comfortable place. Let's picture this: our Shepherd is out front, leading. Beside us is a still stream. It's not raging, maybe it's babbling, but we are teachers, we can handle a little babbling. Behind us are goodness and mercy and on the other side is the rest of the world, our life. Sometimes we turn our head and focus on the world. It draws us toward chaos and confusion. But our Shepherd is good. He pulls us back. His goal is to keep us on the path beside the restful waters.

It's thirty minutes before school. The copier is broken. Someone used the last of the coffee creamer. You get a text asking for two weeks of homework because Joey is going hunting. Ms. M. asks if you can take her duty today. The principal reminds you he wants generic sub plans by 3:00. Oh, where is that still water? School hasn't even started and it's already a raging flood. God doesn't lead you beside the raging flood. Chaos and confusion are not from God.

"YOUR KINGDOM IS AN EVERLASTING KINGDOM, AND YOUR DOMINION ENDURES THROUGHOUT ALL GENERATIONS." PSALM 145:13 ESV

God is sovereign. He has dominion. When it starts feeling like He is not in charge, when there doesn't seem to be a babbling brook in sight, we need to do something about it. Get alone and pray until you sense God's presence. You still won't have creamer and the copier still doesn't work, but now the Shepherd is leading, not the chaos.

Crazy day? Follow Him.

Week 3 Day 5: Gather

"THE LORD BUILDS UP JERUSALEM; HE GATHERS THE OUTCASTS OF ISRAEL. PSALM 147:2

The outcast. Rarely is there a year without one. The kid whose parents are going through divorce; one whose parent is an addict; the autistic child, or the one who is simply different. Sometimes they separate themselves and sometimes the others leave them out. Either way, you feel the need to gather them.

The word *gather* means to enfold or to collect. Gathering is not easy. Sometimes a child resists what he needs most. You want to draw him in and enfold him, but he won't let you. He stiffens with your hug, and his eyes glass over at your words of encouragement.

"O JERUSALEM, JERUSALEM.... HOW OFTEN I HAVE WANTED TO GATHER YOUR CHILDREN TOGETHER AS A HEN PROTECTS HER CHICKS BENEATH HER WINGS, BUT YOU WOULDN'T LET ME." MATTHEW 23:37 NLT

These situations call for us to be consistent and steadfast. You can't force inclusion, but you can improve the situation. As the teacher, you can show honor to an outcast and it can sway the attitude of a class. One year in second grade I made the outcast my teacher's pet. I gave her errands to run and little privileges. After a while the other little girls began to include her on the playground. That was a success story. Building up an outcast doesn't always work but it does show the outcast that you value him. Did you notice in Psalm 147, the Lord first builds up, then He gathers. It's important that every child see they have worth. You very well may not be able to pierce the outcast's armor until you have first built them up. You may have to remove grave cloths before you can make any progress. Have you ever tried to build something with a deck of cards? That's the kind of building and gathering necessary for an outcast. Slow and steady wins the race. If nothing else, by May you will have a child who knows her teacher and her God value her. That can change a life.

Week 4

Week 4 Day 1:
The Night of the Seven Pukes

You've been up all night. Maybe it isn't a puking child, but something has kept you up all night. Not one wink of sleep have you had. Four o'clock rolls around and you can't imagine going into work today. You push the thoughts of sub plans and six a.m. sick calls out of your mind and head to the shower. You will go to school today. You will face those eager faces and plaster on a smile. You will not lay your head down during devotions. You will rally yourself to face the day even though your comfy bed calls to you. Why? Because that's what you do. You're a teacher.

"I CAN DO ALL THINGS THROUGH CHRIST WHO STRENGTHENS ME."
PHILIPPIANS 4:13 NKJV

Through Christ are the key words here. It is only through Christ that you will make it through this day. You are not a normal person who can call in sick when you've had an all-nighter, mopping floors, scrubbing toilets, and changing sheets. You have twenty or so kiddos anticipating a day with you, not some stranger. You know it will upset the ones who count on you for consistency. They've just begun to trust you. So you reach out to grab the hem of Jesus' garment and pray He will drag you through the day. Through Christ, and a little caffeinated help, you will somehow supernaturally make it through the day.

"BLESSED BE THE LORD, WHO DAILY LOADS US WITH BENEFITS."
PSALM 68:19 NKJV

The Lord loads us with benefits. One year a friend and I decided to go tent camping with our four kids. We each had all the things necessary to set up two family camps. We *loaded* all that stuff in my Dodge Expo, which is a little smaller than your usual minivan. Then we piled in. We looked like the Beverly Hillbillies with boxes and tents piled on top and supplies and kids filling every inch of the interior. That's the way the Lord loads us with benefits. Even after a night of seven pukes.

Week 4 Day 2:
Location, Location, Location

"He will be like a tree firmly planted by streams of water."
Psalm 1: 3

We've talked about the steadfastness of being planted. Today let's talk about the location. There is a certain amount of thought that goes into the placement of a tree. Will it get too much sun? Will it block a view? Is it too close to the septic tank? When you plant a tree, you want it placed in just the right spot.

You are the tree planted in this classroom with these kids. It's no accident. Before the foundations of the earth God planned to plant you here. This is where you belong. You have stuff to offer these kids and they have stuff to teach you. Sometimes we wonder if our location is a mistake, "Lord, am I really supposed to be here?" Actually, even if you took a job that wasn't His best plan for you, He knew it all along and already has a plan to bring good from it. That's what He does.

"And we know that God causes all things to work together for good."
Romans 8:28

You are planted right where God wants you. This is not a mistake. If the class is challenging, take James' advice and count it joy. They're making you a better teacher. They're stretching you. You're learning strategies you won't discover with an easy class. You're finding skills you never knew you had. If this class is a dream class, enjoy it and blossom. Consider it a gift from God. Either way, know that you are the Esther of your class for such a time as this.

You are planted. Chosen by God to be right where you are. He contemplated and hovered and planted you. He is with you, tending, pruning, watering, and loving. He is proud of you, proud of your growth, proud that you turn to Him instead of struggling on your own. You are planted.

Week 4 Day 3: Wither

"Its leaf does not wither. In all that he does, he prospers."
Psalm 1:3 ESV

It's the middle of another week and you feel yourself wilting. You have this promise that you will not wither. You might droop a little, but you will not wither.

Yesterday a friend was pulling dead leaves off a plant. The leaves had ceased to do their job. They were no longer nourishing the plant so she plucked them off. You will never reach that point of fruitlessness because the Holy Spirit is in you.

"Whoever believes in Me, as the Scripture has said, out of his heart will flow rivers of living water." John 7:38 ESV

You have a never-ending supply of sap. You will not wither. However, sometimes you feel withered. You pour out until you feel empty. You need to get the sap moving. Set aside the day's plans and do something that brings you joy. Take off your shoes, gather the kiddos around and tell them about a time God moved in your life. Talk about Heaven or the rapture. You will find yourself and the kids getting excited. There is nothing that gets the sap moving like seeing your kids excited about the Lord.

If you feel withered, the kids will sense it. If it's a lesson they aren't getting and you have no more ideas to help them, put it aside. Take a brain break. Pushing through will wither all of you. Even cars on a racetrack take a pit stop for fresh oil now and then.

One last thought on withering. You have the promise that you will not wither but let's look at it another way. Suppose the leaves of your tree are your students. You have the promise that they will not wither! That they will not fall away or fail or be foolish! Now there is something to pray!

Week 4 Day 4: Fruit or Fall

"In all that he does, he prospers." Psalm 1:3 ESV

Stuart doesn't understand rounding. Ayla hasn't asked Jesus in her heart. Bruce didn't get a thing out of the presentation you just did. We look at our day through a microscope, focusing on the failures. But that's what we do. We make the big bucks (sarcasm) to look at lacks and fix them. We stand on chairs and dance on desks. My 4th grade teacher jumped up and down and clicked her heels together for a little guy who finally got 100% on his spelling test. We will do almost anything to reach our kiddos. But sometimes every trick in our Mary Poppins bag seems to fail. Sometimes Stuart moves on to the next grade without understanding rounding. Did you fail? No.

It's autumn and the tree outside my window is beginning to yellow and drop leaves. Is it failing? No. It's doing what it's supposed to do in this season. Do I see any fruit? Nope, just the opposite. I can't go by what I see. But I have faith in what I don't see. In the right season it will bear fruit. What you are doing will eventually prosper. All the desk dancing and Kagin structures, the hours of planning and carrying them out will prosper. Your rhymes and manipulatives that seemed to be failures will reach their season. Yes, the season for fruit will arrive for Stuart. Stuart will round! Oh yes, he will. He may or may not remember that you built the foundation, but that doesn't matter. What matters is that your work prospered! And Stuart prospered! And Beth will ask Jesus in her heart because you planted or watered. And Bruce, well he may never get your presentation but that's ok because he did get that his teacher loved him and went out of her way to help him and that will prosper in him his whole life.

"Then the Lord your God will prosper you abundantly in all the work of your hand." Deuteronomy 30:9

Week 4 Day 5: Invisible Voice

"Then God said, "Let there be light"; and there was light."
Genesis 1:3

God said, "Let there be light," and it actually happened. He spoke and light responded. I think every teacher experiences the invisible voice syndrome. You speak and there is no response. We laugh about it but sometimes it's an indication that something that is not from God has snuck into your room. The enemy does not want your voice heard. He knows the power of the spoken word and he wants to render you ineffective. Now I'll admit there are plenty of times the kids don't listen because they simply don't want to. They aren't interested in the directions for the language exercise and they prefer to have you give them one-on-one help. But if voice invisibility continues and escalates, you may be facing something more than disinterested kids.

"For our struggle is not against flesh and blood, but against the rulers, against the powers, against the world forces of this darkness."
Ephesians 6:12

Many times, while the kids are at recess or lunch, I reclaim my room. I command any forces of evil to leave and I declare that the Lord God Almighty has dominion in my room. I ask the Lord to give the kids ears to hear what the Spirit of the Lord says (Rev 2). When Satan sneaks in and builds a fortress against you in your own classroom you cannot just stand silently by. You must take a stand.

"Then He called His twelve disciples together and gave them power and authority over all demons, and to cure diseases."
Luke 9:1 NKJV

Jesus gave authority to His disciples and all believers. Your voice is to pierce the darkness, not become invisible. It's your job to defend your voice. You are called, anointed, and equipped. Do not allow yourself to be silenced.

Week 5

 # Week 5 Day 1: Forward March

"HIS FOUNDATION IS IN THE HOLY MOUNTAINS." PSALM 87:1 NKJV

These past few weeks you have laid the foundation. Review time is over and you are getting down to the business of building on that foundation—introducing new material! Now the fun begins! After weeks of getting their feet wet, most of the kids have gained the confidence to move forward. They are ready to tackle something new. Of course, there may be a few who will never be ready. Those you gently pull forward like I pull my dog into the vet's office. Either way, with eagerness or tugged on a leash, it's time to move into the real work of your grade level.

"THE EYES OF YOUR UNDERSTANDING BEING ENLIGHTENED."
EPHESIANS 1:18A NKJV

If you haven't already, it's about time to start praying the verse above; for the kids on the leash and for yourself. One of the great things and hard things about teaching is that every class is different. What worked last year might not work with this group. You constantly monitor and adjust, not just daily or moment by moment, but yearly as well. God knows the plans He has for us, but as for our own plans, sometimes they must be thrown out. Maybe this year's class is extra high or extra low or extra unique. Don't let yourself become the Schnauzer on the leash. Be willing to try something new. Let the Lord enlighten the eyes of your understanding. The Lord will give you the key to every group and every child. He has not called you to a locked door. You pray for your kids' understanding and God gives you the key. You become the answer to your own prayer. Suddenly you get a great idea. You think, "Why didn't I think of this before, it's so obvious." You find yourself filled with ideas that don't come from any earthly source, they come straight from the Maker of Heaven and earth. Your understanding is enlightened and in turn, you enlighten your kiddos.

Let your light shine.

 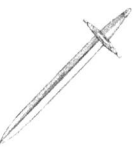

Week 5 Day 2: Shepherding

"I WILL ALSO RAISE UP SHEPHERDS OVER THEM AND THEY WILL TEND THEM." JEREMIAH 23:4A

A pastor once told me, "You're the shepherd of a small flock." He was right. As Christian teachers we are shepherds to a little flock. Sadly, we don't get the tax breaks pastors get. In fact, we spend a lot on our little sheep! But that's okay because we aren't in it for the money.

When the pastor said I was the shepherd of a flock I thought he meant the lambs running around my classroom each day, but later I realized my small flock was bigger than that. The flock we tend includes not just our lambs, but their families as well. Parents are a BOGO for teachers. Buy one, get two free. I've learned over the years that it's crucial to make friends with parents.

Making friends with parents will help you better tend your lambs. Parents are your partners in the educating of lambs. Even if they seem uninvolved, you must treat them as partners. Encourage and build them up, pray for them. Life is hard. Raising kids is harder. I have learned most parents are doing the best they can in the circumstances of their lives. Like it or not, part of your job is to tend them. The Hebrew word translated *tend* means, to pasture, feed, and to associate with as a friend. It's not enough to just tend the lambs. If you're just tending lambs your ewes and rams could be lost. I know the lambs take so much of your time, but the ewes and rams don't need much: a word of encouragement, a laugh over their little lamb, a note, a hug. They are navigating this crazy thing called parenting. Just like you, they're making mistakes and learning from them. You, the shepherd, can make their job a little easier.

"I AM THE GOOD SHEPHERD; THE GOOD SHEPHERD LAYS DOWN HIS LIFE FOR THE SHEEP." JOHN 10:11

Week 5 Day 3: Tending to Business

"I AM THE GOOD SHEPHERD; THE GOOD SHEPHERD LAYS DOWN HIS LIFE FOR THE SHEEP." JOHN 10:11

We are good shepherds, offering our sheep a yummy pasture of educational tidbits; a pasture where they can grow and thrive. We keep them safe from wolves (and often other lambs). We tend and defend them. An aspect of the word tend is, to rule.

"YOUR ROD AND YOUR STAFF, THEY COMFORT ME." PSALM 23:4B

Our lambs are comforted by the order in our pasture. Even though they are often the source of the disorder, our kids crave the security of an orderly classroom. What is the tone of the classroom? Are we respectful? Are our words kind? As the shepherd, you model the tone you want to achieve. Are you enthusiastic but calm? Do you rule the pasture? Are your rules and procedures clear and consistent? Those qualities, like a rod and staff, produce comfort to the kiddos. Often their home life is a whirlwind of homework, dinner, and sports. Your classroom may be the only calm point in their day. Your rod and your staff allow for fun engaging learning but not chaos.

"HE RESTORES MY SOUL; HE GUIDES ME IN THE PATHS OF RIGHTEOUSNESS FOR HIS NAME'S SAKE." PSALM 23:3 NASB

When chaos erupts, you need to restore the soul of the room! Guide the kids back to the order and peace they really want. You are a good shepherd. You don't allow the sheep to go crazy. Your day has purpose. You have goals to meet. You can't waste time on chaos. Interestingly, the word *chaos* means waste and confusion. Your lambs need calm, order, comfort, and purpose. They need you to guide them in paths of righteousness. When you rein them back in, you are doing the right thing. They will bleat but don't take it to heart. You are the shepherd. It's your job to tend.

Tend to business.

Week 5 Day 4: Hallowing

"Pray then, in this way: 'Our Father who is in heaven, Hallowed be Your name.'" Matthew 6:9

To hallow means to venerate. It's a good idea to stop now and then and ask ourselves, how are we doing at hallowing? Noah hallowed God with steadfast obedience. Abraham hallowed God with faith. Esther hallowed him with courage. Zaccheus hallowed by new-found integrity. These Bible heroes displayed evidence of their hallowing attitude. I'm not talking about evidence of things not seen, I'm talking about evidence that was very evident!

"Create in me a clean heart, O God; and renew a right spirit within me." Psalm 51:10 KJV

The pull of the world is strong. We find wonderful ideas on the internet. Teacher's stores are full of bright shiny, glorious things for our classroom. What do these things lift up? The limited ingenuity of man! The other day I looked around my room to see if it hallowed God. I was disappointed in myself; very little pointed to the Lord I needed a right spirit renewed in me. I wanted my room, as well as my life, to blatantly hallow the name of God—in neon lights! We can't accomplish that without a right spirit.

What if Noah had built the ark hidden away deep in the forest? Technically he'd be obedient, but would he be hallowing God's name? What if Zaccheus started following Jesus but didn't make reparations to the people he cheated? Would that hallow God's name?

Yes, put Bible verses on your bulletin boards but a right spirit does more! A right spirit finds ways to hallow God all through the day. The evidence of our attitude toward God should be blatant in all we do, not just displayed on a wall. A great way to incorporate hallowing is through an anticipatory set. Start lessons by targeting God and refer back to Him throughout the lesson.

"In all your ways acknowledge Him." Proverbs 3:6

Hallow His Name.

Week 5 Day 5: Thy Will Be Done

"Your kingdom come. Your will be done, On earth as it is in heaven."
Matthew 6:10

This section of the Lord's Prayer isn't so much a prayer as it is a declaration. Jesus is declaring God's kingdom and will, much like God's declaration, "Let there be light." In order to obtain a right spirit, in order to hallow God's Name in our life and classroom, we need His Kingdom and will. We need to seek it first and often. Our students need to understand that prayer isn't just a list of requests. It is also declaring God's will and Word over situations.

In her Mitford series, Jan Karon refers to "Thy will be done," as the prayer that never fails. What a door we open when we pray that!

"Power and might are in Your hand so that no one can stand against You." 2 Chronicles 20:6b

Nothing can stand against God's kingdom and will. That is a powerful weapon we can wield from God's Word. One year a man was placed in a position of authority over our school. He wasn't a proponent of Christian education. Our staff began to pray fervently. We weren't praying against him, we were praying for him—for God's will in his life and ours.

"The Lord moved the heart of Cyrus king of Persia."
2 Chronicles 36:22b NIV

If the Lord could move a king's heart on behalf of the people, He can move the heart of someone trying to stand against you. It wasn't long before the man we prayed for began to see some benefit to our ministry. God moved his heart. God's kingdom came and His will was done.

The Lord's prayer is Jesus' model to show us how to pray. We teachers get that. We model things every day. Along with the academic concepts we model for our kids, we need to model our trust in God. We need to hallow His name and call for His will in front of our kids. They need to see evidence of our trust in God. As they see us model a relationship with Christ, His kingdom will come, His will shall be done.

Week 6

Week 6 Day 1: Conference Time

"And walking in the fear of the Lord and in the comfort of the Holy Spirit, they were multiplied." Acts 9:31 NKJV

I want to tell you about my first parent teacher conference as a parent. I eagerly went in to hear what the teacher had to say about my wonderful little kindergarten boy, my first and only child at that time. Nothing good. Not one good thing did she say about my sweet boy. He didn't sit still, he bothered other children, and on and on. Did she mention that he could read and write? That he knew his numbers and colors? No. I was crushed.

When I became a teacher myself, I determined I would never do that to a parent. Parent-teacher conferences are not the time to drop bombs. If a little booger can't sit still, don't wait till conference time to tell the parents. If you are having a problem with a child, call the parents in to work out a solution early on.

"But speaking the truth in love." Ephesians 4:15a KJV

As Christians we are called to speak truth in love. Love. Whatever we share at a conference, it must be clothed in love.

"Death and life are in the power of the tongue." Proverbs 18:21a NKJV

Let's be sure we speak words of life. Not every bit of information you need to tell the parents will be pleasant, but it must be said with love. Remember you are partners this year. Always start your conference with prayer so you are assured of the Lord's active presence in the meeting. Always give the parents an opportunity to speak and always listen. And, you know this but I'm going to say it anyway, *always end on a good note.*

Week 6 Day 2:
So

"For God so loved the world, that He gave His only begotten Son." John 3:16 NASB

I was thinking about the word "so," wondering why God put it there. So, I looked it up. It means, "in this way." Our verse could be written, "God, in this way, loved the world." Then it gives an example of the way He loved the world, "that He gave His only begotten Son." He loved the whole world so much, He gave what was most precious.

Let's apply this verse to teachers. "For the teachers loved their class in this way, that they gave…" What is it we give because of our love for our class? The first thing that comes to my mind is time. Time in the summer planning and preparing and taking classes. Time in the evening and weekends grading, planning, and preparing. Time on "breaks" and holidays. Oh! And what about the time you spend getting ready for a sub if you take a day off? It is often time away from your family, time away from your church, your friends, your hobbies, your sleep, even time to use the restroom. Yes, teachers definitely give their time because they so love their class.

What else? Teachers give the fruits of the Spirit. I remember driving home from school and telling my family, "I had a bad day, don't expect anything from me." All my fruits of the Spirit were used up, poured out. I had given all the fruit in my basket.

We give of our finances. We give of our sanity. We give more love than we knew we had. Why? Because that's what we do. Because we love our class and we love teaching. Is it a sacrifice? Do we suffer? Sometimes. Is it worth it? Absolutely. In thirty-some years of teaching rarely have I ever met a teacher who considered teaching a job. It's a calling, an identity; it gives our life purpose. It's our very being.

So (in this way) we hunt for standards, we set goals and objectives, we jump through educational hoops and swing with educational pendulums because it's worth it. We constantly work to improve what we do because we *so* love.

Week 6 Day 3: Cling-ons (Klingons)

"For God so greatly loved and dearly prized the world that He [even] gave up His only begotten (unique) Son, so that whoever believes in (trusts in, clings to, relies on) Him shall not perish." John 3:16 AMPC

I love the Amplified version of this verse. There are plenty of days we feel like we might just perish! Those are the days we must cling-on.

"She had heard the reports about Jesus, and came up behind him in the crowd and touched his garment." Mark 5:27 ESV

Maybe it's the weather or the candy someone handed out. Maybe it's the full moon or Bobby's birthday, or javelina loose on the playground. Whatever the reason, your class has become a mob and you are on the verge of perishing. Those are the days we must reach out, grab hold of Jesus' robe, and hang on for dear life.

"For I am convinced that neither death nor life, neither angels nor demons ... nor anything else in all creation, will be able to separate us from the love of God." Romans 8:38–39 NIV

Neither weather nor candy nor even wildlife on the playground can separate you from the love of God. When the atmosphere of the classroom becomes chaos you must do something to change it. Step one is to reach out and cling on to Jesus. Maybe you stop and pray with the class, maybe you step in the hall to get ahold of His garment, or maybe you just throw Heavenward a silent plea for help. Somehow you have to disconnect yourself from the chaos and connect with your Peace.

Step two is to change what's going on. Do something different. Sing a song, Google *Brain breaks for kids*, take an extra recess, do a class building Kagan structure, or just read aloud to them. This step is so obvious but sometimes when we are in the midst of chaos we forget. We get wound up right along with the kids and we forget to take a deep breath and reach out to our Peacemaker. Once we get hold of our Peacemaker, we can become a peacemaker.

Week 6 Day 4: Let It Go

"For God so loved the world." John 3:16a NIV

God gave Jesus because of His love for the world. What in the world do you love? Show your students what you love. Be contagious about those things. Let them see your authentic love for the Lord. You may be the only genuine Christ-lover in their life. Share your testimonies. Be excited for theirs.

"And you must commit yourselves wholeheartedly to these commands that I am giving you today. Repeat them again and again to your children. Talk about them when you are at home and when you are on the road, when you are going to bed and when you are getting up." Deuteronomy 6:6–7 NLT

What else do you love? Family? Talk about what your family does. Let them know you have a life outside of school. You're planting seeds in the hearts of some who need to see what a healthy family is like. What about church? Do you love your church? Talk about how important it is in your life.

Share your passion for everything Jesus. I am a Disneyland fan. Everyone who knows me knows I am. Hopefully everyone knows I love Jesus even more. Be contagious about what you love. Do you love dogs? World War II History? Narnia? Let your passion loose. When you introduce your students to your passions you are enriching their lives. My 4th grade teacher loved birds. We read about Audubon, studied all kinds of birds, drew birds, and learned how to care for birds. Birds weren't necessarily in the 4th grade standards; she just loved birds. To this day I love birds too. She was contagious.

"I am fearfully and wonderfully made." Psalm 139:14b

God made you unique just as He has your kiddos. You are a teacher with certain loves and bents that God intends you to share with your students.

Let it go!

Week 6 Day 5: Fresh

"It will be healing to your body And refreshment to your bones."
Proverbs 3:8 NASB

Isn't it amazing how tired you can be Friday morning and how fresh you become at 3:00? Thursday night you are too tired to do anything and Friday night you're ready for some fun.

It's crucial to find refreshing on a regular basis. If you don't, you'll burn out. It can't always be Friday, so we have to find other ways to get refreshed.

I live in Arizona where it's nice and dry. One time I had a package of graham crackers that had been left out on a rare rainy day. They became slightly soft. I meant to throw them out but just didn't get it done. A couple sunny days later they were crisp and fresh again! Like my crackers, it doesn't take much to make us fresh again. Many times, just stepping out of the classroom after school and visiting with other teachers is refreshing. Yet how many times do we tell ourselves we don't have time to visit? We have papers to grade, pages to copy, sanity to scrape off the floor. Allow yourself some time to decompress with your coworkers. They need it too.

"Then Israel sang this song: 'Spring up O well.'"
Numbers 21:17

When your well is dry you need rivers of living water to spring up. Spend some time with the Lord. Put on your favorite praise music. Get your favorite coffee. Go to a movie, play a game, call an old friend. These are quick, easy and cheap ways to get refreshed.

"Dry bones, hear the word of the Lord!" Ezekiel 37:4 NIV

If you want your teaching to have life, if you want to impact the lives of others, you cannot allow yourself to become dry bones. Taking time to refresh is an investment. It will pay off with longevity in your career. It will pay off with sanity.

Week 7

Week 7 Day 1: Grace

I just spent an hour doing long division with a struggling student. By the end of our hour it seemed like she understood less than when we started. Instead of two steps forward, one step back, it was one step forward, two steps back. But I'm not discouraged. One thing I've learned in thirty years is: grace works.

"MY GRACE IS SUFFICIENT FOR YOU, FOR MY STRENGTH IS MADE PERFECT IN WEAKNESS." 2 CORINTHIANS 12:9 NKJV

This verse is written in red. It's not in the gospels—but it's written in red. These words are so important Jesus spoke them from Heaven. They are some of the last red words so they must be pretty important. *Jesus' grace is sufficient.* We do what we can do, then step back and let grace do its work. I'm not saying give up. No. Tomorrow I will spend another hour on long division. I'm saying don't put all the responsibility on your shoulders.

"BE STRONG IN THE LORD AND IN THE STRENGTH OF HIS MIGHT."
EPHESIANS 6:10

All the training, experience, and ideas we possess are not the limit of what we have to offer. There is more to us than earthly abilities. We have grace, and part of that grace is the strength of God's might. Let's look at this verse in the classic Amplified version.

"DRAW YOUR STRENGTH FROM HIM [THAT STRENGTH WHICH HIS BOUNDLESS MIGHT PROVIDES]." EPHESIANS 6:10B AMPC

Boundless. We have boundless help. We do what we can and God makes up the difference. In one of my early years of teaching I had a little girl who was struggling to read. We kept plugging along, doing all I knew to do, praying for grace. Today she is a wonderful teacher. Success wasn't because I did the right thing, it was because neither of us gave up and both of us trusted the Lord to intervene.

As Winston Churchill said, "Never give in. Never give in. Never, never, never, never—in nothing, great or small, large or petty—never give in."

And when you've done all to stand; stand. Stand trusting in the grace Jesus promised.

Sufficient grace.

Week 7 Day 2: Betwixt and Between

"So Moses arose with Joshua his servant, and Moses went up to the mountain of God." Exodus 24:13 NASB

Joshua and Moses left the camp to go up the mountain. Somewhere along the way, Moses posted Joshua to wait while he went on alone to the mountain top. There, the cloud of God's glory rested upon the top of the mountain for six days. On the seventh day, God called to Moses. Those down in the camp said God's glory looked like a consuming fire. Moses entered the cloud of God and remained there forty days and nights. What about Joshua? What do you imagine he was doing? I think he was probably doing a little hunting, and a lot of praying. Forty days and nights all alone on the side of a mountain. Above him the fire of the Lord was burning bright, below him were his friends and family.

Do you ever feel like Joshua? Located between God and your family in a sort of twilight zone? Spending your days doing your all-out best to serve God, and your family doesn't really get or appreciate it? You're pouring out your heart and soul to serve the Lord and you have family members who resent your service? Those who have never taught just don't get it. They don't understand how consuming teaching is. In the early August school prep days, even after 30 years of marriage and the same number of years teaching, my husband would say, "What do you do up there all day?" Ouch! Just twist that knife a little more!

Joshua was chosen to serve Moses and to succeed him. We are chosen as well. Chosen by God to teach. God held out to us the gifting to teach and we reached out and accepted it. Not everyone understands or appreciates our gift but that's okay. We know God is just up the mountain. He knows and loves us. He appreciates our heart to serve Him and our students. He understands sometimes it is a sacrifice.

Week 7 Day 3: Rainy Day Recess Again?

"Be gracious to me, O God, according to Your lovingkindness." Psalm 51:1

No matter how your school handles rainy days, it seems to upset the apple cart. Rain alone stirs kiddos up, and if you add wind to it, forget about all you hoped to accomplish. Then having to stay inside all day? Well, you have apples rolling helter skelter all over the place. How do you hang on to your sanity?

"Have I not commanded you? Be strong and courageous! Do not tremble or be dismayed, for the Lord your God is with you wherever you go." Joshua 1:9

Don't let yourself be dismayed. The way I see it, you have two choices: get them worn out with some indoor exercise or get them calm with peace and quiet. If you planned a new cooperative learning activity and it lands on a bad weather day, you might want to adjust your plans. Cooperative learning isn't always cooperative on days the wind is blowing.

When you find yourself fighting a losing battle, when you are nothing but negative, it's time to redirect. Trying to push through with your plans is going to make everyone miserable and will accomplish nothing in the end. You tell yourself, "I'm so far behind, I have to get this done today!" But you are just spinning your wheels. You've heard of DEAR: Drop Everything And Read. Maybe it's time to DEAP: Drop Everything And Pray! The Lord will give you ideas and DEAR might be one of them. Let your plan go. It's not going to happen and you'll just waste your good plans by trying to force them. Try again tomorrow. Get out the multiplication bingo, do a craft, play board games, review, brainstorm, write. The Lord will make up the difference for you. He knows your situation.

"Then He will give you rain for the seed which you will sow in the ground ... and it will be rich and plenteous." Isaiah 30:23 NASB

Week 7 Day 4: End Each Day Well

"I press on toward the goal to win the prize for which God has called me." Philippians 3:14 NIV

A great tip I received as a young teacher was to end each day well. The very experienced teacher who gave me the tip said, "Do something fun at the end of the day and the kids will think they've had fun all day."

"Oh, give me back my joy again; you have broken me—now let me rejoice." Psalm 51:8 NLT

In nearly every class we have kiddos who feel broken for most of the day. They struggle with reading or math which is the core of a school day. School can become one failure after another. Day after day they pound on a brick wall of frustration. Even if you do lots of engaging activities they feel like the tail end of a game of crack the whip, hanging on for dear life. But if your day ends with a crazy song or dance, or a fun game, you will send your little strugglers home with a happy heart.

At one point in Moses' trek around the wilderness, the Israelites were very thirsty but the only water in the area was bitter. This reminds me of our strugglers. They come to school thirsty to learn but the outcome is often bitter. Moses cried out to God and was shown a tree. He threw it in the water and the water became sweet. Doing something fun at the end of your day can make a bitter day sweet; not only for the kids but for you too.

Let the end of your day be a prize the kids press on toward. Make it something they look forward to through the day, during long division or deciphering pages in the Science book. Let it be a light at the end of a tunnel.

"Weeping may last for the night, But a shout of joy comes in the morning." Psalm 30:5b

Or vice-versa. Joy comes at the end of a well-planned day.

Week 7 Day 5: The Double Portion

"Elisha picked up Elijah's cloak, which had fallen when he was taken up." 2 Kings 2:13 NLT

This is a familiar story. Elijah is taken up to heaven in a whirlwind. His cloak falls off, the cloak symbolic of his anointing. Elisha picks up the cloak and receives a double portion of Elijah's anointing. He knew he'd need more than his own skills to carry out the job set before him.

Admittedly, I am an older teacher, an Elijah. I've had a wonderful anointing for nearly forty years. My anointing was effective and sufficient. You are most likely Elisha teachers who are taking the baton we pass. We drop the cloak of our anointing for you to pick up.

The other day I was wondering, *what if Elisha hadn't picked up the cloak?* Would he have survived with only his own single portion anointing? Would there have been miracles without Elijah's anointing? Did Elisha actually have a triple anointing? His own plus the double portion of Elijah's?

Teachers today need more than a single portion anointing. You are daily dealing with situations I couldn't have imagined in my early years of teaching. You need more than your own skills to carry out the job set before you. You need to pick up the double portion cloak. You need a supernatural anointing.

"You (Moses) shall put some of your authority on him (Joshua), in order that all the congregation of the sons of Israel may obey him." Numbers 27:20

The supernatural anointing is available to you just as it was for Joshua and Elisha. Do you take extra vitamins and herbs during cold and flu season? Of course you do. If you didn't, your immune system would be weakened and you wouldn't be able to teach effectively. The same is true in the spiritual realm. You need to pick up that double portion every morning. You need to bulk up, double layer your cloak of anointing.

"And the Lord opened the servant's eyes and he saw; and behold, the mountain was full of horses and chariots of fire all around Elisha." 2 Kings 6:17

Go for the double portion.

Week 8

Week 8 Day 1:
Steps

"I WILL GIVE YOU EVERY PLACE WHERE YOU SET YOUR FOOT."
JOSHUA 1:3 NIV

Often I like to start my school day by walking the perimeter of the room. I sing a praise or worship song, or just say the name of Jesus over each desk. Just as you hovered over your room getting ready to start the school year, you have to continue hovering. Every step you take, God will give you dominion.

"BE STRONG AND COURAGEOUS, BECAUSE YOU WILL LEAD THESE PEOPLE TO INHERIT THE LAND." JOSHUA 1:6 NIV

To maintain the positive atmosphere of your room, there are steps you can take. In the first chapter of Joshua we find the steps God taught Joshua.

1. Be strong and courageous. God tells him this three times and the second time He says be *very* courageous. When God repeats something like this, He is serious. We must not let ourselves be intimidated by circumstances. Difficult child, parent, or coworker? Be loving, respectful and kind, but don't be intimidated. You have the mind of Christ and are filled with the Holy Spirit.

2. Obey the law. God is referring to His law. Do things God's way. Be light and salt, show God's love, and do what is right in God's eyes.

3. Do not let the Book of the Law depart from your mouth; meditate on it day and night. The Bible is a supernatural living book. It has the power to speak to you, correct you, convict you, encourage you, edify you, and more. It's important to be in the Word daily. If you sense the atmosphere in your room declining, read God's Word out loud. Find an appropriate passage and declare it. Think of the Bible as spiritual water. It sustains life.

4. Do not be fearful or discouraged. This is a crucial step. Fear and discouragement are not from God. They are fiery darts the devil uses to penetrate our thoughts. We must not accept them. They will rob us of courage and strength. Resist the devil, make him flee.

Victors take steps. We set our feet. We don't back down.

Week 8 Day 2: Goatheads

"AND AS FOR THOSE WHO DO NOT RECEIVE YOU, AS YOU GO OUT FROM THAT CITY, SHAKE THE DUST OFF YOUR FEET." LUKE 9:5

I have a schnauzer who has fur like Velcro. He walks across the floor and leaves a trail of leaves and goatheads. If you're not familiar with goatheads, they're a type of bur with steel spikes. If you step on one, you know it!

We also pick up undesirable stuff as we go through our day. We visit with those who are critical and we come away grumpy ourselves. We have a student who's disrespectful and we're left offended. A student suddenly takes a dive and we can't figure out what's going on; confusion and frustration cling to us. By the end of the day we look like a pin cushion. We started our day fresh and pleasant, but we end up grumpy and frustrated. What happened? We collected all the junk thrown at us.

"TAKE UP THE SHIELD OF FAITH, WITH WHICH YOU CAN EXTINGUISH ALL THE FLAMING ARROWS OF THE EVIL ONE." EPHESIANS 6:16 NIV

Flaming arrows of evil, the perfect description of goatheads. It's also a great description of what happens to us through our day when our shield is down. Notice Paul says, "take up" the shield. It isn't always there. We must grab it and hold it up. When we encounter criticism, we must lift our shield. We must intentionally deflect the critical spirit. If we're not careful, goatheads of criticism will penetrate our spirit. Like the dust on the disciple's feet, we must shake it off.

Not only must we defend ourselves from goatheads, we must be careful not to be contagious. My dog leaves goatheads in rugs for me to step on. He's a good sharer. The goatheads we fail to remove impact the atmosphere of our class. Our attitude rubs off on the kids. Before you know it, there's a room full of grumps.

Lift your shield, shake off the goatheads, and let the Spirit rise.

Week 8 Day 3: The Town Crier

"The math is too hard. I don't understand the reading. My chair squeaks. You won't help me enough. You help me too much. No one will play with me at recess." *Of course no one plays with you, you cry all the time!*

"Sir," Gideon replied, "if the Lord is with us, why has all this happened to us? And where are all the miracles our ancestors told us about?... The Lord has abandoned us and handed us over to the Midianites." Judges 6:13 NLT

Whine, whine, whine. Gideon must have been a crier. It's bad enough with all the complaining, but the sobbing! Ugh. What do you do about that? One year there was a student next door who sobbed so loudly she was often sent to the hall. There she would turn up the volume and disturb my whole class! I'm not very sympathetic to the town criers.

Sometimes this is how they cope. Like people who giggle when they're nervous. Criers are often just doing what comes natural to them. Other times criers are needing attention. Perhaps at home they only get attention when they cry. Some criers just need a hug or a pat on the back; a little show of affection calms them down. Whatever the reason, we can't let them disrupt the classroom.

"The angel of the Lord appeared to him and said, 'Mighty hero, the Lord is with you!" Judges 6:12 NLT

How did the Lord handle His crier? He came near and pointed out Gideon's potential. He reminded Gideon he wasn't alone, that God was with him. Even though Gideon continued to doubt, the Lord didn't argue, He kept encouraging; telling Gideon he was strong and able and that he had purpose.

Somewhere along the line our little criers need to learn to handle their frustration appropriately. Pointing them to the Lord and reinforcing their potential will help.

"Those who plant in tears will harvest with shouts of joy." Psalm 126:5 NLT

Hang in there and stock up on tissues.

Week 8 Day 4: Do I Love Them?

You're nearly a quarter into your year and you're worried because you don't really love these kiddos. You miss last year's kids whom you loved and knew so well. But this class? Will you ever love them?

Whether it's a hard class or a joyful class, eventually you will love them. It happens every year. You worry, but somewhere along about Christmas you will realize, "Hey, I love these kids!"

"LOOKING AT THE MAN, JESUS FELT GENUINE LOVE FOR HIM. 'THERE IS STILL ONE THING YOU HAVEN'T DONE,' HE TOLD HIM. 'GO AND SELL ALL YOUR POSSESSIONS AND GIVE THE MONEY TO THE POOR, AND YOU WILL HAVE TREASURE IN HEAVEN. THEN COME, FOLLOW ME.'" MARK 10:21 NLT

Jesus was facing a spoiled, entitled young man. And yet He felt genuine love for him. It's a supernatural thing. God puts *His* love for people in our hearts. One year I had a boy with a severe behavior disorder. He caused nothing but trouble. But I loved that boy, still do. He pushed me way out of my comfort zone, but I loved him. The Lord put His love in my heart. It's not love "by faith" where we confess we love them when we really don't. It's genuine love.

"O JERUSALEM, JERUSALEM!… HOW OFTEN I HAVE WANTED TO GATHER YOUR CHILDREN TOGETHER AS A HEN PROTECTS HER CHICKS BENEATH HER WINGS, BUT YOU WOULDN'T LET ME." MATTHEW 23:37 NLT

Jerusalem was not always loveable. It was full of Pharisees, hypocrites, and enemies of Jesus, but He loved them. The only way it was possible was the supernatural love of God.

Rarely do we experience love at first sight with a class. Love grows over time. God will help you love them all because "For God so loved the world He gave…" (John 3:16 KJV)

You will come to love this class, even the little stinkers.

Week 8 Day 5: Clamor

"Let all bitterness and wrath and anger and clamor and slander be put away from you, along with all malice." Ephesians 4:31

You're going through your day. It's getting louder and louder in your room. You find yourself shouting and still not being heard. As time passes you get more and more frustrated till you're at your wit's end.

"Trust in the Lord with all your heart, And lean not on your own understanding." Proverbs 3:5 NKJV

At your wit's end you will find the Lord. Recently, in a roaring classroom, at my wit's end, I heard the Lord say, "Look around." I stopped trying to yell over them and did just that. The kids were doing what they were supposed to be doing. They had pleasant looks on their faces. There was no angry shouting except for mine. Where was the noise coming from? I realized many of them were making senseless noises, weird hums, buzzes, etc. I asked the Lord what was going on and He said, "Clamor."

Clamor is a loud continuous noise going on and on. Sound familiar? Clamor in the classroom is common these days, even with the best classroom managers. Clamor is a weapon of the enemy. Isn't it interesting that clamor is grouped right along with bitterness, wrath, and anger? We easily recognize these as tools of the devil. But this chaotic din? We've become numb to it. Isn't it just the way kids are today?

"Stand against the schemes of the devil." Ephesians 6:11 ESV

Spiritual warfare is necessary to fight clamor. Yes, use your management techniques, but this battle is going to take more than earthly techniques. It requires weapons that have "divine power to destroy strongholds" (2 Cor. 10:4 ESV). Clamor is a stronghold. Our verse says to let clamor be put away from us. We must put on our full armor of God and kick clamor out of the room. Get friends to help, don't give in. Jesus leads us in triumphant victory. What do we pray? Pray the opposite of the weapon Satan uses. Pray peace, quiet, still waters, rest, calm.

You can do this!

Week 9

 # Week 9 Day 1: Calming the Clamor

"Let all bitterness and wrath and anger and clamor and slander be put away from you, along with all malice." Ephesians 4:31

As I was praying for friend who's dealing with an extreme case of classroom clamor, I thought about the kiddos in her room. There are a few who are quiet and peaceful. I've had their siblings and I know that these kids come from peaceful homes. They have parents who are very involved and love Jesus. These kids go home to parents who generally interact with them in a positive, constructive way. Sadly, many of the students participating with clamor do not go home to peace. They rush to activities, rush to do homework, rush to shovel down supper, and rush to bed. Many of their homes are filled with unfortunate situations resulting in tension and stress. Their lives are full of clamor.

One year I had a fourth grader who brought a stuffed animal with her everywhere she went. Many kids bring clamor with them like a stuffed kitty. How do we get them to check it at the door? One thing is to set the atmosphere of the room before the kids arrive. Make it a daily practice to invite the Holy Spirit into the room. Play soft worship music, unless it adds to the clamor. Use your weapons. 1. The name of Jesus; it's the name above clamor. 2. The Bible; God's Word is powerful and effective. Again, speak it. "Lord, lead us beside still waters today. Give us clean hearts and right spirits." 3. Prayer; go around the room and pray over each child as the Lord leads.

You can slay this giant.

 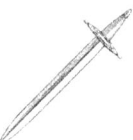

Week 9 Day 2: Gideon and the Clamor

"These enemy hordes (Midianites), coming with their livestock and tents, were as thick as locusts; they arrived on droves of camels too numerous to count. And they stayed until the land was stripped bare." Judges 6:5 NLT

Gideon was dealing with clamor. He's in a winepress avoiding the Midianite clamor, doing the least he can possibly do, eking out a meal or two while his mind is whirling. Clamor has overtaken him. But the Lord comes, calls Gideon a mighty warrior, and gives some great advice for battling clamor. "Go in the strength you have…. Am I not sending you?" (Judges 6:14 NIV). The Lord sees a strength in you. Something clamor cannot conquer. You will persevere and bring this clamor into order.

"So Gideon built an altar to the Lord there and called it The Lord Is Peace." Judges 6:24 NIV

One of the first things Gideon did was bring in the presence of the Peace. He built an altar to God then pulled down the altars of the false gods. Is there anything in your room that adds to clamor? Walk through the room and ask the Lord if there is anything that doesn't please Him. If He brings anything to your mind, don't argue about it, get it out of your room. You are in a spiritual war; you don't want anything in your room that welcomes the enemy. Have the kids clean their desks and take home any trinkets you don't feel good about. The Holy Spirit will guide you.

Is your room over stimulating? This is a problem of mine; I like lots of bright cheerful things on my walls. It might be a good idea to take down what's not necessary. Not because it's bad, but simply because it encourages clamor.

"And do not give the devil a foothold." Ephesians 4:27 NIV

You are in a battle for the souls of your children and for your own sanity. Pray and declare God's Word. Mountains will move in the unseen realm.

Go in the strength you have.

Week 9 Day 3: Report Cards

"Martha, Martha ... you are worried and upset about so many things." Luke 10:41 NIV

Whether we are a Martha or a Mary, at quarter end we must all be Marthas! Extra hours of grading, getting plunkers to turn things in, entering grades, making sure there are no surprises, writing report card comments. There are so many things to worry about. And oddly, the world doesn't stop so we can do this. We still have our normal duties. Martha, Martha, Martha!

As I look over my kid's grades, I always ask myself if the grade reflects their ability and effort. If it doesn't, I take a closer look. Did I make a mistake? If not, but the grade seems wrong, I need to find out why and prepare the parents ahead of time. Never, never drop a bomb. Be sure you make time to look over the reports before they go out.

Take a little Mary time; pray about your comments. The report card should reflect the child and it should also reflect you. When the parents look over their child's report will they see harsh grades with no grace, or will they see deserved grades tempered with words of encouragement? Even plunkers have God-given gifts. It's hard, but I know you can find something good to say. Ask the Lord. Don't make something up but find some genuine encouragement for every kid.

"But speaking the truth in love, we are to grow up in all aspects into Him who is the head, even Christ." Ephesians 4:15

Kids always want to know what the teacher wrote on their card. They want to know what we see in them, if we love them. The report card is not the place for, "Bobby needs to get his work turned in on time." That belongs in a personal note or phone call. When Bobby is 52 and finds his old report card, wouldn't it be nice if it said, "Bobby prays lovely prayers," or "Bobby is quite an artist."

It's Martha time but let's be sure to add a few drops of Mary too.

Week 9 Day 4: Haunted/Hounded

"You prepare a table before me." Psalm 23:5a

It's nearly Halloween and I am being haunted. Haunted with questions, "Can I do this? Do I have what it takes?" Haunted with condemnation, "You can't do this. You don't have what it takes. You should not be teaching." Doubts and condemnation are not from God. They are tools to make you ineffective in the work God has gifted you to do.

When you go to the dentist, the assistant comes in beforehand and lays out all the tools the dentist will need for your procedure. She prepares a table before him. Everything the dentist needs (plus more) are on that table.

God has prepared a table for you. Every tool you need for a successful school year is on the table, both natural and supernatural. A dentist has very specific tools for his trade. God has given you very specific tools for your trade. While dentists generally use all the same tools, teachers do not. The tools on your table are different from the tools on your neighboring teacher's table. Don't condemn yourself and don't compare yourself. God has prepared a table specifically for you and your class. Next year He'll prepare a new table before you and it might include different tools. David's tools included stones and a sling. Gideon's were pitchers and torches. God prepared a table for each of them.

You do have what it takes. God has placed before you everything you need. Some of it you learned in classes, some of it comes from the Holy Spirit. I was a pretty new Christian when I got my first teaching job. I remember telling the Bible stories. Wisdom and great applications would come to me as I was teaching. I was lacking but my table was full.

God's grace is sufficient, and His mercies are new every morning. So you had a bad day, reach out to the table. Grab some new mercies. Pick up your sling and stones—ok, maybe not stones, stones are probably not on your table. Grab what you have been given and start fresh with no hauntings.

Week 9 Day 5: Hovering, Again

"Then God said, 'Let lights appear in the sky to separate the day from the night.'" Genesis 1:14a NLT

A new quarter is beginning and it's time to hover again, time to do some separating. If you haven't rearranged the desks already, it's time. It takes a lot of hovering to move desks because there is such a crazy domino effect. Puff can't sit by Sally, Jane annoys Tabby, and so on. It's like putting together a jigsaw puzzle. So we hover, separating the day from the night. It's tempting to leave the day and night where they are, but you've noticed that Jimmy Day is wearing thin of Bobby Night. You can't reward his patience by making him endure another quarter of Bobby.

It's also time to mark the season. We hover over autumn, trying to minimize Halloween and accent Thanksgiving. As much as we might like to, we cannot ignore Halloween; so we find ourselves again trying to separate day from night. How can we vindicate this holiday? It's a selfish holiday, all about getting. Let's attack it with the opposite of getting, giving! Perhaps collect school supplies for a public school with low income families, or socks and mittens for a local homeless outreach, or diapers for a crisis pregnancy center. Let's mark the season by developing something valuable in our kiddos, a heart to give. Why not provide opportunities for them to be light and salt at Halloween?

It's the quarter end and you hover. You rearrange your kids, you aim them toward a more Christ-like focus. Now, what about you? How are you doing? What was good about this first quarter? What do you want to do different next quarter? What do you need to rearrange or target in your own life? In the days between last quarter and next quarter why not take some hovering time for yourself? Go to a favorite spot, get a special treat. Look back and look forward. Don't look at failures, just successes and dreams. Let God refresh you.

"Let me prepare some food to refresh you before you continue on your journey." Genesis 18:5 NLT

Week 10

Week 10 Day 1: Looming

It's a bright shiny Monday morning but you look toward Friday with dread. The week is looming in front of you. You have so much packed into this week, you are overwhelmed before you even start. And much of it has nothing to do with educating the kiddos in your class! An assembly, perform in chapel, be observed, and present a lesson in professional development. That's on top of all the usual. Oh, and then there's home: birthday party, football game, science fair project, on and on. Your week hasn't started, and you want to climb back into bed.

"BUT THERE THEY ARE, OVERWHELMED WITH DREAD, WHERE THERE WAS NOTHING TO DREAD." PSALM 53:5A NIV

You feel like giving up before you start. Don't do it. Don't focus on your full plate, just eat your peas. You didn't do this to yourself; most of the things on your plate were put there by others. God knows what's on your plate and that you didn't choose it all.

"HE MAKES EVERYTHING WORK OUT ACCORDING TO HIS PLAN." EPHESIANS 1:11B NLT

God is with you. He will work it all out. Can you imagine how Joshua felt as he stood looking at the walls of Jericho? Walls so high and thick, houses were built on them? Joshua didn't focus on the walls, he looked up. And what did he see? God was there ahead of him. And He had a sword in His hand. The Lord was not overwhelmed, He was ready. He had Joshua's back and He has yours.

Joshua knew his help came from "the Maker of Heaven and earth." You have the same helper. Don't look at the long week looming in front of you, just take the first step—and then take the next step. Look up above the mountains where your help comes from. That's pretty good help! Help that can do far abundantly beyond what we can imagine. Help that gives us strength. Help that enables and equips us. Help that refreshes and renews and makes us young again. Help that can bring down walls we just walk around.

Week 10 Day 2: Interruption

You are marching along through your day and suddenly God interrupts. He was there all along, but this is different. Suddenly you realize the Holy Spirit is doing something. The all too familiar Bible story has been struck by lightning. The glazed look in the kid's eyes is replaced by a spark. Everyone is sitting up, listening up, hands up.

"BUT YOU WILL RECEIVE POWER WHEN THE HOLY SPIRIT HAS COME UPON YOU."
ACTS 1:8

Do you stick to your schedule and plans? You could do that of course, but what a sacrifice. The teacher in you may scream, "Stay on task, move on, you don't have time for this." But this is a teachable moment. Lives may be touched by the power of God. Math might be missed but hearts may be touched.

In these situations, we can be Cain or Abel. Cain leans on his own understanding and sacrifices this intimate moment with God in order to stay on schedule and get Language done before recess. Vegetables. Not the sacrifice God desires. Abel offers God free will. Freedom to reach your students' eternal hearts. Teacher Abel knows his day is going to be messed up, but he also knows this moment is going to be defining in the lives of his students. These interruptions are the things kids remember when they are out of school and thinking through the deep doubts and decisions of life.

"AS HE WAS TRAVELING, IT HAPPENED THAT HE WAS APPROACHING DAMASCUS, AND SUDDENLY A LIGHT FROM HEAVEN FLASHED AROUND HIM."
ACTS 9:3

Saul had an agenda: go to Damascus, find Christians, bring them bound to Jerusalem. His agenda was interrupted. It was really an inconvenient interruption, but it impacted not only Saul's life, but yours and mine.

When that interruption comes, that sudden light from heaven, let's step back and see what God can do.

"YOU NEED NOT FIGHT IN THIS BATTLE; STATION YOURSELVES, STAND AND SEE THE SALVATION OF THE LORD ON YOUR BEHALF." 2 CHRONICLES 20:17

Week 10 Day 3: Parents

"You prepare a table before me in the presence of my enemies."
Psalm 23:5

As a young teacher I considered parents an imposition. Over the years the Lord has renewed a "right spirit within me." I now understand that the parents and teacher are a team. The problem is, some parents don't realize it. As teachers we have to find a way to work together.

Enemy Parents. The most difficult parents are the ones who are always looking for you to make a mistake. They eagerly look over the graded papers and newsletter hoping to find something you did wrong, a way to discredit you. Somehow you are the bad guy and you don't know why. Most likely these parents are not mature parents. The good thing is, they keep you on your toes and working hard to be salt and light!

Helicopter parents. They do everything for their child and expect you to do the same. They don't want their child to experience anything uncomfortable—no consequences for their kiddo. Consequences are the best teachers. Consequences birth compassion and humility. Helicopter parents would have skipped the forty years in the wilderness and taken their kids right into the Promised Land. They are more concerned about how their kids feel than who they are. But, they have a good side too. They will be on every field trip and will help when you need help, and they will produce some lovely projects. Focus on their good points. They can be a blessing or a thorn in the side. It's your attitude toward them that decides which. Just understand, you will not change them.

The teachable parent. I'm going to skip the rest of the types of parents who are difficult (we could write a book) and move on to the teachable parent. What a breath of fresh air! You are not the enemy. They value your input. They listen. They read your newsletters and overlook your mistakes. They know their child isn't perfect. They bring you coffee. Thank God for these parents who keep you going and encourage you and remind you why you do what you do.

Week 10 Day 4: No Common Interest

I've been watching a show about a Gold Rush. People from all over rushed to Canada, traveled together over horrible terrain, and carried heavy supplies in order to find gold. There were pictures of hundreds of people in a line, climbing over boulders in mountain passes. Even though they were lined up tightly, the commentator said they had "no common interest." They weren't a team, they weren't there to help each other. It was every man for himself.

There are times we feel like Klondike Stampeders. We are surrounded by people but all alone. It's hard for teachers to develop relationships with coworkers. We are so crazy busy we don't have time for relationships.

Almost no one in your life shares more common interests than the teachers you work with. The teacher who had your class last year knows what you are going through. She has insight and encouragement you need. Isolating is only hurting yourself and your students.

"They devoted themselves to the apostles' teaching and to fellowship, to the breaking of bread and to prayer. All the believers were together and had everything in common." Acts 2:42,44 NIV

The believers in Acts devoted themselves to fellowship and having everything in common. What can you do to promote common interest and fellowship? I had a pastor's wife who asked our Bible study to write three encouraging notes a week for the duration of the study. None of us were crazy about it but we were obedient. I began to write notes to the teachers at my school. Guess what? They wrote back! Something so simple as receiving a note from someone with common interest lifted our spirits. Nothing is as encouraging as a sincere note from someone who knows what you're going through. It's a nice habit to start.

Fellowship is more than a note, though, and it's more than following someone up a mountain for the gold at the end. Fellowship is joining hearts and hands and pulling each other up that mountain. Sharing the common interest.

Surviving and thriving.

Week 10 Day 5: Hang On!

Some years it feels like we're riding the roller coaster of Joseph's life: in a pit, out of a pit, sold as a slave, nice owner, tricked and thrown in prison, favor with warden, met the king's butler, he forgets him. Our plans and hopes rise then suddenly fall.

"Hope deferred makes the heart sick." Proverbs 13:12a NIV

In a roller coaster year we must hold on tightly to hope. Joseph's hope could not be fastened to the hand that pulled him out of the pit or the favor of Potiphar or the promise of the butler. His hope, and ours too, must be fastened to true and eternal Hope.

"I lift up my eyes to the hills. From where does my help come? My help comes from the Lord, who made heaven and earth."
Psalm 121:1-2 ESV

Many times in the story of Joseph we read, "The Lord was with Joseph." In the pit, in slavery, in prison, and as a leader in Egypt, the Lord was always with Joseph. When things are going well, or poorly, the One who created heaven and earth is your help too. Whether you're teaching in person or from home, whether your wonderful plans fall apart or succeed, you have this amazing Helper that you can confidently fasten your hope to.

"The Lord was with Joseph, so he succeeded in everything he did."
Genesis 39:2 NLT

You are destined for success. When things look bad, God works things together for good. His ability to help has no limit. You can fasten your hope on that! In a roller coaster year, hang on and watch what God can do.

Enjoy the ride.

Week 11

Week 11 Day 1: Squirrel!

"Finally, brethren, whatever is true, whatever is honorable, whatever is right, whatever is pure ... dwell on these things." Philippians 4:8

One morning I hit a squirrel on the way to school. I called to my daughters, "Don't look back!" I didn't want them to see the squirrel. I knew if they looked, they'd be haunted by pictures of a dead squirrel.

As teachers, we can't be focusing on dead squirrels. It's hard to drag your eyes away from roadkill, but you must. Bobby is so messy, Alice never has her work done, Jim is late every day, and Becky doesn't smell very good. These things can become dead squirrels, things you can't ignore, things that cause a rift between you and your kiddos. You cannot focus on things the kids can't help. It's not easy when your room reeks of cat pee.

Gideon was like a dead squirrel. He hung out in a wine press—sounds stinky. He was dirty from standing in grape mush, beating out wheat; the least of the least. Awkwardly he demanded a fleece and then another one. He feared his father's household. Squirrel! But the Lord saw beyond the junk. He saw a mighty warrior.

Your Gideons need you to see the mighty warrior in them. They need you to see their potential. Just as the Lord overlooked Gideon's flaws, you look above to see the gifts and talents in your little squirrels.

"Look, God is all-powerful. Who is a teacher like him?" Job 36:22 NLT

God, who is a teacher, has equipped you as a teacher. He has not made you a Pharisee, He has patterned you as a teacher after His own heart. He made you and He made your squirrels. He will help you both.

"The Lord has today declared you to be His people, a treasured possession." Deuteronomy 26:18a

Treasure, not roadkill.

Week 11 Day 2: Rushing

The holiday seasons are quickly approaching. Seasons so packed with activities, projects, and programs, there is barely time to breathe. You feel driven to rush.

In the Bible, the word *rushing* never refers to God rushing His people. God is not a God who rushes you. Would He have Joshua walk around Jericho seven days if He was rushing? No, He'd have him run around once and call it good. Would He lead His people around the wilderness forty years if He were rushing? Of course not. God doesn't rush His people. There's always a purpose in process and delay. So why this naggy urging to rush all the time? Why are you discouraged and disappointed as you feel yourself falling behind? Those symptoms are not from God. They might be from you setting expectations too high or they might be from the enemy. Remember God's yoke is easy. Even if He asked you to rush, it would be accompanied by grace and peace, not the heavy burden of condemnation. The nagging voice telling you, "hurry up, get busy" is meant to derail you. It's ironic that the urging to rush is really a tactic to slow you down.

"BUT THEY WHO WAIT FOR THE LORD SHALL RENEW THEIR STRENGTH."
ISAIAH 40:31A ESV

It's waiting that renews your strength. Of course the enemy wants you to rush. He wants you weak and weary. God wants you out of the rat race and growing in Him. He has plenty of plans and plenty of time to accomplish them. God unfolds His plans a little at a time. Do you dump your groceries on the counter all at once? Probably not; most likely you unload them one or two items at a time. God doesn't dump all His plans at once. You wouldn't expect your students to learn a year's worth of knowledge in a season. Plans take time. Rushing produces poor results.

Slow down. Enjoy the season.

Week 11 Day 3: Lying Lips

"Save me, Lord, from lying lips and from deceitful tongues."
Psalm 120:2 NIV

Is there any teacher in the world who hasn't thought this, especially after recess? The mob comes in from the playground, voices raised over some altercation, "Tom cut in the kickball line." "Junie B. let me cut." "It was my turn to pitch and Jill wouldn't let me." "Sam was bullying me."

"Oh Lord, save us from the lying lips!"

This psalm is the first of a group of psalms called Psalms of Ascent. Some say they were psalms repeated as pilgrims ascended the steps to the temple. It's interesting the first step deals with lying lips. One of the least enjoyable aspects of teaching is figuring out who is telling the truth and who is lying when the accuser of the brethren comes visiting. Oh, if only everyone told the truth, the job would be so much easier!

But lying kiddos are not the only liars you have to deal with. "You shouldn't be a teacher." "You're so far in debt, you'll never get out." "Those symptoms you have are serious." Fear. Fear can be a constant liar, whispering in your ear day and night. Have you ever said to a student, "I'm sorry, I don't believe you?" That is what you need to say to the lying lips of fear. "I don't believe you. My God supplies all my needs. He is my healer, my provider, my equipper, and more."

"Hold up the shield of faith to stop the fiery arrows of the devil."
Ephesians 6:16 NLT

Whether the lying lips are from kiddos in your room or Fear having a heyday in your mind, you must stop the lie. Don't allow lying lips to rob your classroom time. Unless it's very serious, it's better to deal with it at the next break. The opposite is true of Fear. Don't give it time to fester, use God's Word and boot it out of your thoughts right away.

"Resist the devil, and he will flee from you." James 4:7b NLT

Make fear flee.

Week 11 Day 4: Help!

"I lift my eyes to the hills. From where does my help come? My help comes from the Lord, who made heaven and earth."
Psalm 121:1-2 ESV

This is the second psalm of ascent. The second step up. The first step was about quenching lying lips, like cleaning and decorating your room for a new season. Step one, clear out the clutter; something good is coming. Step two, lift your eyes. When you rid yourself of lying lips, you can focus on truth; your helper is God. Wow! The end. What could be better? This is only the second step out of the fifteen psalms of ascent. It seems like this should be the top step. But instead it's foundational, a step the rest of the steps are built upon. Step one, stop listening to the devil. Step two, look to God.

God is your help. When things are crazy at home, when you're asked to chair the Christmas Parade float committee, when a church friend needs to talk, when Stuart can't even remember the letters in his name, God is your help.

"But you are a chosen people, a royal priesthood, a holy nation, God's special possession." 1 Peter 2:9a NIV

God is watching to help you. He looks around and says, "Who shall I help today?" And the answer is "you." You, who He chose. You, God's special possession. Not only that, He has also chosen the kiddos in your class. The little one who comes in late every day—from a crack house. God is his helper. And the kiddo who never appreciates anything and is so entitled, God is her helper too.

In the fractions and fragments of our lives, God is our help. Have you ever taken a field trip to one of those pizza places that has games? The kids play the games and earn points to trade in for little prizes. When it comes time to select their prizes it takes FOREVER. God stood before the showcase of eternity and didn't hesitate a second. He chose you and each of your kiddos. And why? So He could help you. The Maker of heaven and earth wants to help you! Wow! What a comfort.

Week 11 Day 5: Beautiful Feet

"How beautiful on the mountains are the feet of those who bring good news." Isaiah 52:7a NIV

As you climb the mountain of this school year your feet might not always feel beautiful but in the spiritual realm they are. As you stand and move about your room you are spreading good news in so many ways.

Bible time is the most common time to spread good news. You work hard to make it impacting and relevant. You pray, tell the Bible story with great finesse, share a testimony, and give opportunities for life application. Your feet are beautiful.

Do you have a place in your house where everyone keeps their shoes? My grandma always kept her galoshes beside the back door. Beautiful feet don't leave the good news in one place, they bring it everywhere. The Lord interrupts your Language or Reading class and turns the focus to Himself; not every day, but when He does, your feet carry those messages. You give Him the stage, you allow His interruption. That makes your feet beautiful.

Moving through your forest of busy workers you stop and whisper a word of affection or encouragement. Even if it's the kind of compliment they tell us not to give: "I love your shirt!" A shallow, non-character trait compliment still communicates that you notice, that you care. Beautiful feet.

You hoped to get out of Walmart without any interaction, but your beautiful feet run into a school cutie. Even though your hair isn't washed and you have paint on your shirt, you smile and hug and show the love of Jesus. You pat the head of baby brother with the green runny nose and visit a bit with mom. You share your humanness. And when your beautiful feet move away you leave that weary mom with the cart full of kiddos feeling a little better about herself.

"Who proclaim peace, who bring good tidings, who proclaim salvation, who say to Zion, 'Your God reigns!'" Isaiah 52:7 NIV

Your God reigns. And your feet are beautiful.

Week 12

Week 12 Day 1: Love Like a Mom

You're busy decorating your room for Christmas. There is so much to do. And the cherry on top of this busyness is your concern to focus the kiddos toward Jesus. How do you trump Santa and the Elf on the Shelf? It's a yearly struggle. How do you make a story they've heard hundreds of times fresh and interesting? Maybe by relating freshly to it yourself.

"BUT MARY TREASURED UP ALL THESE THINGS AND PONDERED THEM IN HER HEART." LUKE 2:19 NIV

This year I've been thinking how, as a mother, Mary treasured Jesus even before He was born. She was willing and committed from before conception. A mother's love is a good way to love Jesus.

My daughter recently had a baby. She prepared before his birth, knitting her heart to his in her womb, and has completely turned her life upside down for him. Every decision my daughter and son-in-law make centers around their precious baby. Every room in the house is changed for their little guy: the kitchen is a bathing station, the living room looks like an infant workout room with all sorts of equipment, the bedroom contains everything one might possibly need to make it through the night. And the spare room? Well, there is no spare room, it's David's room.

Baby David has acid reflux. It's nothing serious, but many days of his five months have been uncomfortable and sad. It's not been easy for mommy and daddy. But when the days were long and hard, did Sarah give up on him? No, because she loves like a mother, completely committed to him, no matter what.

What better way to love Jesus than like a mother, fully committed, life altered, unconditional love. Isn't it how we want our kiddos to love Him?

"AND THIS IS MY PRAYER: THAT YOUR LOVE MAY ABOUND MORE AND MORE IN KNOWLEDGE AND DEPTH OF INSIGHT." PHILIPPIANS 1:9 NIV

And this is my prayer: that this Advent season you may impart your love of Jesus to your students and together may your love for Jesus abound.

Treasure Him.

Week 12 Day 2: Ragged

"A MAN WAS GOING DOWN FROM JERUSALEM TO JERICHO, WHEN HE WAS ATTACKED BY ROBBERS. THEY STRIPPED HIM OF HIS CLOTHES, BEAT HIM AND WENT AWAY, LEAVING HIM HALF DEAD." LUKE 10:30 NIV

Do you ever have those days? You feel stripped, beat, and half dead?

When we read the story of the Good Samaritan, we usually focus on the three men who encountered the victim. Today, let's look at the victim. He probably got up early, packed his teacher bag, grabbed his lunch and coffee, and headed out the door for his journey to Jericho. He had plans, an objective, and I'm sure he even had standards! Somewhere along his well-planned, well-intentioned day, something went wrong. Maybe the administrator dropped in. Maybe there was a full moon or wind. Whatever the reason, our friend went from confident traveler to victim in the ditch.

"WHO REDEEMS YOUR LIFE FROM THE PIT AND CROWNS YOU WITH LOVE AND COMPASSION." PSALM 103:4 NIV

The Lord never leaves us in the ditch. Maybe our day ends up in the ditch but it's a temporary situation.

"HE WENT TO HIM AND BANDAGED HIS WOUNDS, POURING ON OIL AND WINE." LUKE 10:34 NIV

My first year of teaching, I cried every night. I felt so inadequate, like I was failing. I didn't have it in me. But every morning I couldn't wait to get back to class and give it another try. Somewhere between sunset and sunrise Jesus rode up on His donkey and treated my wounds. I went from victim to victor. How? Time spent with Him.

No matter how stressful our day, how much is piled on our plate, or how ragged and beat up we feel, we must reach out to our Samaritan. Neglecting time with the Lord will leave us bleeding and dying on the Jericho road. We think we don't have the time or energy to read the Bible and pray. However, that is exactly what we need. Jesus restores our soul, but only if we reach out to Him.

Jesus, give me CPR.

Week 12 Day 3: Glimmers

Day after day we teach the stories of the Bible. We plan practical applications, model God's love, sing about Him, and demonstrate how to pray. We do everything we know of to encourage our kiddos to love God.

"SO THAT YOU, YOUR CHILDREN AND THEIR CHILDREN AFTER THEM MAY FEAR THE LORD YOUR GOD AS LONG AS YOU LIVE." DEUTERONOMY 6:2 NIV

We want our kids to have a vibrant relationship with Jesus. We don't want to produce shallow, self-righteous Pharisees.

"I PLANTED, APOLLOS WATERED, BUT GOD GAVE THE INCREASE."
1 CORINTHIANS 3:6 NKJV

Our student's salvation is not on our shoulders. We teach, apply, model, sing, and of course, pray, but it is God who is ultimately responsible for their spiritual condition. We do all we can, but we do not fret. We are part of a team. There are sowers and waterers who go before and after us. God takes the pieces each of us submit, puts them together and brings increase. The hard part about being on this team is that we may not see the results of our efforts.

Once in a while though, God gives us a little glimmer. One year our state was struggling financially. The Governor declared a state day of prayer. My class and I spent some time on our knees praying for the economy. At the end of the prayer time a little girl came up to me and said she felt the Lord wanted her to read a Bible verse. It was Psalm 34:6: "This poor man called, and the Lord heard him; he saved him out of all his troubles." It was a perfect verse and encouragement. Her parents, church, and school were sowing and watering her little soul and the Lord was bringing increase.

While we can't always see the results of our labors, we can be assured that our faithful God is always blessing our work and bringing increase.

"AND BEING FULLY ASSURED THAT WHAT GOD HAD PROMISED, HE WAS ABLE ALSO TO PERFORM." ROMANS 4:21

We are not alone. Watch for the glimmers!

Week 12 Day 4: Wrestling

"Epaphras,...is always wrestling in prayer for you, that you may stand firm in all the will of God, mature and fully assured." Colossians 4:12 NIV

Oh, my goodness. Do we ever wrestle for our little darlin's! For nine months these are our kids. The same as a pregnancy. We are birthing a year of school in them. We're teaching, nurturing, coaching, disciplining, molding, shepherding, and wrestling. For nine months they are part of our being. I have met teachers who were able to go home and forget about their students, but those teachers are rare. Most of us take our kids home, to the store, to church, and even on break. In fact, we take them into our hearts for a lifetime. I bet if you stop right now you can think of a former student you're still wrestling for.

"Each one had a harp and they were holding golden bowls full of incense, which are the prayers of God's people." Revelation 5:8b NIV

Year after year we wrestle in prayer. Many times, we don't see the victory or even an answer. But our job is not to worry about the answer, our job is to wrestle and give it to God. Imagine yourself wrestling a big heavy box into the post office. You hoist it up on to the counter and turn it over to the postmaster. You don't have to wrestle it into the back room, onto a truck, drive the truck to the destination. You do your part getting it to the post office and putting it in the hands of the experts. Our prayers are held in golden bowls. At the right time, the answer will be delivered. We can count on it.

"The prayer of a righteous person is powerful and effective." James 5:16b NIV

Week 12 Day 5: Doubting Thomas

"Unless I see the nail marks in his hands … I will not believe." John 20:25b NIV

Nearly every year we have an unbeliever in the class. The kid that always asks, "What if…?" You lay down the clear black and white of a subject and their little hand shoots up, "But what if…?" I can't even tell you how many times I've said, "No 'what ifs!'"

I wonder if the Lord feels that way when we doubt Him?

"My God will meet all your needs according to the riches of his glory." Philippians 4:19 NIV

We think, *Really? But what if I don't deserve it? What if He doesn't consider this a need?* Does God want to say, "No 'what ifs!'"

As teachers we are filled with what ifs. What if I offend a parent? What if mister A student suddenly earns a B? What if these kiddos never learn long division? What'll I do, oh what'll I do? Many times I heard the Lord say, "Just trust." Is it really that simple? It is. But just because it's simple doesn't mean it's easy. Do you remember the scene in Indiana Jones where he had to cross a narrow invisible bridge? He threw some gravel out in front of him and then he could see the bridge. That's what our trust is often like. We take a deep breath and throw it out there and take a step or two. Doubt, worry, and fear make the path invisible. Trust is a handful of gravel.

"Trust in the Lord with all your heart and lean not on our own understanding." Proverbs 3:5 NIV

Trust is throwing out that handful of gravel knowing God is with us. One hand throws gravel, the other hand grabs the hem of His garment, and off we go. "What if…God turns a heart, gives the wisdom He promises, does abundantly more than we could ask or imagine?" What if we trust instead of doubt?

Week 13

Week 13 Day 1: Patriotism

I'm a big Disneyland fan and one of my favorite things is the flag retreat. Everyday just before sundown the Disneyland band marches down Main Street USA to a patriotic tune. At the flagpole the band plays the songs of each branch of the military and they call for veterans and soldiers to step forward to be honored. Then comes the Star Spangled Banner and the flag is lowered and folded. I cry every time. One year a young veteran of Afghanistan walked up to a WWII Veteran in a wheelchair and thanked him for his service. Every time I watch this ceremony my heart swells with pride for my nation.

"NOW IF YOU OBEY ME FULLY AND KEEP MY COVENANT, THEN OUT OF ALL NATIONS YOU WILL BE MY TREASURED POSSESSION." EXODUS 19:5 NIV

Our nation is a treasure. How do we teach our kiddos to be patriots? How do we make them treasure this soil they run on each day? How do we help them realize how important it is to pray for our leaders, soldiers, and missionaries? Like with so many other things, we model it. Say the Pledge of Allegiance with enthusiasm and make sure they understand it. Collect pictures of soldiers and national leaders to pray for. Sing patriotic songs. Read patriotic stories and books. Learn some of the famous speeches and documents of our nation. Make patriotism a part of your class standards.

As we come up on Veteran's Day and Thanksgiving, let's be contagiously patriotic. Find out about the kids' family members or friends who served in the military and give them an opportunity to share. It becomes more personal to them, gives a sense of national pride.

"I URGE ... THAT PETITIONS, PRAYERS, INTERCESSION AND THANKSGIVING BE MADE FOR ALL PEOPLE—FOR KINGS AND ALL THOSE IN AUTHORITY, THAT WE MAY LIVE PEACEFUL AND QUIET LIVES IN ALL GODLINESS AND HOLINESS." 1 TIMOTHY 2:1–2 NIV

Praying for our nation is a priority. Let's be sure we are raising up Christian soldiers who love the country God has given us.

Week 13 Day 2:
One, Two, Three, Eyes on Who?

"I WILL LIFT UP MY EYES TO THE HILLS—FROM WHENCE COMES MY HELP?"
PSALM 121:1 NKJV

I recently spent three days in first grade. It seemed like I was constantly trying to get the kiddos' attention. I didn't want them fixated on their neighbor's transgressions or the fly on the ceiling. I wanted them to listen and look at me. The Lord wants the same from us. He doesn't want us distracted by annoying mandates that come down the pike. He doesn't want us focused on what's wrong. He wants us focused on Him—the One who can help. All the things that frustrate us are best dealt with by Him.

"BUT AVOID FOOLISH CONTROVERSIES AND GENEALOGIES AND STRIFE AND DISPUTES ABOUT THE LAW, FOR THEY ARE UNPROFITABLE AND WORTHLESS."
TITUS 3:9

If you disagree with mandates or the people around you, your best course is prayer. Prayer will either change your circumstances or change your heart. We are told to seek peace and pursue it. Complaining is destructive. It causes division and strife, not peace. It may feel like prayer is not enough. You feel like you want to do more. Beware. That was the attitude that caused Moses to strike the rock when he was instructed to speak to it. You are also instructed to speak to the Rock: pray.

Remember, our God can turn the heart of a king and do exceedingly abundantly more than we could even imagine. One, two, three, eyes on Him. It doesn't rhyme but it will change your school.

Week 13 Day 3: Growth

"The righteous will flourish like a palm tree, they will grow like a cedar of Lebanon." Psalm 92:12 NIV

This quarter of the school year is about growth. We introduce new information and the students begin to really grow, like a palm tree or a cedar. I read a little about palms and cedars. Both palms and cedars are mainly focused on strength and upward growth. That's exactly what we want for our kiddos. We want our kids to flourish, not only academically but spiritually as well. Just as we laid the foundation for our year with review last quarter, we most likely also laid a spiritual foundation by giving our students an opportunity to receive Jesus. This quarter we focus on growing beyond salvation to developing Christ-like character.

"I press on toward the goal for the prize of the upward call of God in Christ Jesus." Philippians 3:14 ESV

Like palms and cedars, we focus upward. We look for practical applications in our Bible lessons. We seek to find the character of God in the stories of the Bible. We endeavor to make God real and relevant in the everyday lives of our kiddos.

Let's talk a bit about flourish. In Hebrew the word *flourish* refers to budding, blooming, and springing up. That's exactly what this quarter is all about. Our little seedlings are planted and now we begin watering, we throw open the curtains and let in the sunshine; the fun begins! They send down roots and push up buds. They ask thoughtful questions that reveal growth and understanding. They relate Bible stories to their own lives. We see fruit from our labor.

"But grow in the grace and knowledge of our Lord and Savior Jesus Christ." 2 Peter 3:18a

This is only the beginning of tremendous growth this year. Don't worry if you can't see it, roots go down first. Remember to have faith, the evidence of things not seen. Growth is happening whether we see it or not.

"Commit your works to the Lord And your plans will be established." Proverbs 16:3

Week 13 Day 4: Ears to Hear

"He who has an ear, let him hear what the Spirit says."
Revelation 2:29

Our students have ears, but they don't always hear. In fact, we often feel like our voices are invisible. Students today have so much more to distract them; we wonder if they hear or remember anything we say. Don't get me wrong, I'm not being critical of them. I love my kiddos, but Houston, we have a problem.

"The Lord came and stood there, calling as at the other times, 'Samuel! Samuel!' Then Samuel said, 'Speak, for your servant is listening.'"
1 Samuel 3:10 NIV

The word listening is from a Hebrew word that means both hear and obey. It's hearing with the intent to obey. If our students don't listen to us, who they see, how will they be able to listen to invisible God? I love cooperative learning opportunities. I use them all the time. But how do we teach the kids to hear the still small voice without active engagement?

I was talking to a little girl the other day and it was obvious she was hearing the voice of the Accuser. Every word from her mouth was accusation and offense. I prayed with her and asked her listen for the Lord but sadly, all she could hear was the clamor of the Accuser.

"Beloved, do not believe every spirit, but test the spirits to see whether they are from God, because many false prophets have gone out into the world." 1 John 4:1

Along with all the new tasks we, as teachers, are asked to do, teaching our kids to discern the voice of God is the most crucial. We must give them opportunities to listen and express what they hear. We must teach them to listen to the gentle voice of God and resist the naggy voice of Satan. Our little palms and cedars must grow ears to hear.

Week 13 Day 5: Very Present Help

"God is our refuge and strength, A very present help in trouble."
Psalm 46:1

God is not ordinary help, He is very present help. *Very* means exceedingly, and *present* indicates sufficient or enough. Our invisible God is exceedingly above sufficient help. There is no use trying to think of what God might do to help us in a troubled situation because it's going to be much greater than our little pea brains could think up.

One year the church who sponsored our school selected a new pastor. He was a very nice man but without vision or desire for a Christian School. One of his first acts as pastor was to close our day care center. This was very alarming for the school staff. We began to walk the campus and pray. We hardly knew how to pray. This pastor was very good for the church, so we had to pray cautiously. We ended up focusing on the following verse.

"For the Lord had caused them to rejoice, and had turned the heart of the king of Assyria toward them to encourage them in the work of the house of God, the God of Israel." Ezra 6:22

If God could turn the heart of a king toward His people, surely He could turn the heart of a pastor. Honestly, we just hoped the school would be allowed to squeak by. But God is not a squeak-by kind of guy. He showed himself to be very present. Not only did the pastor eventually embrace the school and become our school pastor, but he found an amazing principal for us. It was during this pastor's tenure that our school experienced growth, prosperity, and unity with the church.

As Christian schoolteachers, we will always experience trouble; we are on the front line of the battlefield for the next generation. The solution for every bump or mountain of trouble is our very present Help.

"My help comes from the Lord, who made heaven and earth!"
Psalm 121:2 NLT

Week 14

Week 14 Day 1: Shake It Off

"And wherever they do not receive you, when you leave that town shake off the dust from your feet." Luke 9:5 ESV

Nearly every time my dog gets up from a nap, he takes a moment to shake. I think it's a good idea to stop and shake it off now and then. When our life get crazy and we are ready to throw in the towel, when our mind is bombarded with critical, negative thoughts, it's time to shake it off.

"Wake up, wake up, O Zion! Clothe yourself with strength…. Rise from the dust, O Jerusalem. Sit in a place of honor. Remove the chains of slavery from your neck, O captive daughter of Zion." Isaiah 52:1–2 NLT

Shake off the dust, wake up, change your clothes, and rise above. Our feet trod the dust but our head needs to rise above. I once had a dream of a little frog in a mud puddle. His entire body was in the mud except his eyes; his eyes looked up. The Lord impressed to me that we are like the little frog. We live in a fallen muddy world, but we focus not on the mud, we look up.

It's easy to become embroiled in the recess drama, the heartbreaking prayer requests, the little one who won't ever shut up, ever. But we are called to shake that off. We are called to look up.

"Looking unto Jesus, the author and finisher of *our* faith." Hebrews 12:2a NKJV

My dad built musical instruments. I remember watching him hold the neck of a violin he was finishing. He would carve and sand then stop and blow the wood dust off. As Jesus finishes our faith, the dust must be removed. Imagine His pleasure when we recognize our dusty condition and shake it off ourselves.

Shake it!

Week 14 Day 2: Author

"Fixing our eyes on Jesus, the author and perfecter of faith."
Hebrews 12:2

If you have taught for a few years you have probably begun to worry about the spiritual condition of your students as they leave your class and move on. Too often our sweet little first grade prayer warriors move on to become crude joke tellers. The hearts that were tender toward the Lord seem to become calloused or at best, indifferent. We wonder what happened and how can we stop it?

We must remember we are sowers and waterers in the faith business. Jesus is the author and perfecter. The word *author* here is more about authority than writing books. The verse is saying Jesus is the chief authority leading us on our faith journey. He is also the perfecter of our faith, the completer and finisher.

My daughter recently hired a man to remodel their bathroom. A few days before the project was complete, the man was called away on another job. My daughter has a beautiful new floor, a new toilet, shower, and vanity, new drywall and paint. But the room is not complete. There are no lightbulbs in the fixtures, no trim along the floor, and one faucet is missing. My daughter's finisher and perfecter has abandoned her.

We are not the author or perfecter of our students' faith. We are workers who work for the chief leader. My daughter's contractor had men who did drywall, men who did plumbing, electricians, framers, and so on. Each did their part in the remodel of the bath. Similarly, we are a part of our students' faith journey. We have a responsibility to do our part, but we are not in charge of their faith and we are not the finisher. We do our part and trust the Finisher to bring completion.

As we watch our kiddos become adults and have successes and make mistakes, we can trust the Author and Perfecter to do His job and continue His work.

Week 14 Day 3: Nurture and Admonition

"And, ye fathers, provoke not your children to wrath: but bring them up in the nurture and admonition of the Lord."
Ephesians 6:4 KJV

Let's tear this verse apart a bit. We are going to focus on the positive part of the verse starting with the word fathers. Thayer's definition includes: one who has infused his own spirit into others, teachers. "Bring them up" means nourish to maturity. Nurture in this case means instruct and correct. Finally, admonish means to exhort or a mild rebuke. It all sounds a lot like what we do. Paul instructs those of us who infuse their spirit into children (teachers) to love and feed, instruct and correct, and exhort and rebuke the kiddos in our care.

Year after year we are given a fresh batch of cookies to stir and shape and bake. We bring them along in the nurture and admonition of the Lord. Not just nurture, not just admonish. And not just on our own, but with the Lord. I'll admit I tend a little more to the nurture side and other teachers tend a little more to the admonish side, but if we all bring them up in the Lord, it will balance out. The little one who is often admonished for her spontaneous unbridled behavior also needs to know we love her. On the other hand, we can't be afraid to say wrong is wrong. There is black and white, wrong and right. Pussyfooting around an issue, bending the truth or avoiding it, creates confusion in the kids and results in mediocrity. When we avoid admonishing by putting a positive spin on everything, we are disobeying the directive of our verse. There are no white lies or gray lies. Sin is sin and it's always wrong. Disobedience is sin and needs to be admonished. Yes, we are grace based and I certainly prefer to hand out grace, but we must not exclude admonition.

"But speaking the truth in love, we are to grow up in all aspects into Him." Ephesians 4:15

Nurture and admonition. Truth in love. Anything less is hypocrisy.

Week 14 Day 4: Blessed Assurance

"And being fully assured that what God had promised, He was able also to perform." Romans 4:21

It's one of those days where we wonder if we are really called to teach. If we are going to make it through the rest of a long year, we need assurance. As teachers we are good at thinking up questions that lead to conclusions. What questions should we ask ourselves that will lead us to full assurance? How can we test the spirit behind our feelings? First let's ask what exactly are we feeling? Is it discouragement? Frustration? Weariness? Heaviness? None of these are from the Lord. They are either a result of living on the earth, or a tactic of the devil to remove us from our ministry. When Abram left the comforts of the city of Ur, it wasn't because of anything negative. It was because he heard a clear call of God. He looked forward to the next thing God had for him. He didn't leave Ur like a whipped puppy but in eager anticipation to see what God had planned. Discouragement is not from God.

Moses had several career changes in his life. He left his prince job out of confusion.

"For God is not a God of confusion but of peace."
1 Corinthians 14:33a

Moses took control of his own life instead of waiting for God. He spent forty years in the wilderness due to his decision to act out of confusion. His second career change was from shepherd to national leader. This time he got a clear call from God; a talking, burning bush is clear assurance. Even then, he didn't jump right in. He was cautious to be sure it was God. With a clear call Moses moved forward. When He got discouraged he called out to the One who called him and received assurance and help.

If we doubt our calling to teach, we need to hear from the One who called us. If God is moving us on, He will make it clear and it will not be because we can't handle it. He enables and equips, remember?

Week 14 Day 5: Sorting Assurance

Yesterday we talked about questioning our calling. We asked ourselves what are we feeling that causes us to doubt? Usually the doubts come from circumstances the enemy uses to drag us down. Today's question is, what do we do about the feelings? First, what are we feeling? Discouragement, frustration, lack. Figure out what it is and where it's coming from. Is it a spiritual attack?

"SUBMIT THEREFORE TO GOD. RESIST THE DEVIL AND HE WILL FLEE FROM YOU." JAMES 4:7

Next, fight. Submit your thoughts to God. Resist negative thoughts. Physically push them away if necessary. As I've mentioned before, get a team of people praying for you. Grab someone to pray through your classroom. Listen to what God is saying. Embrace what the Word says. *My God will supply all my needs. I can do all things through Christ. I am wonderfully and fearfully made.*

"FOR THE GIFTS AND THE CALLING OF GOD ARE IRREVOCABLE." ROMANS 11:29

When God called you to teach, He equipped you and made plans for you; He didn't set them aside. He fulfills His plans. Sometimes His plans include a difficult child, a difficult class, or a difficult home situation. But along with those plans are strength and help to handle it.

"NO TEMPTATION HAS OVERTAKEN YOU BUT SUCH AS IS COMMON TO MAN; AND GOD IS FAITHFUL, WHO WILL NOT ALLOW YOU TO BE TEMPTED BEYOND WHAT YOU ARE ABLE, BUT WITH THE TEMPTATION WILL PROVIDE THE WAY OF ESCAPE ALSO, SO THAT YOU WILL BE ABLE TO ENDURE IT." 1 CORINTHIANS 10:13

God will always provide a way of escape. Take some positive action in the physical realm as well as the spiritual. Take a few days off and do something you enjoy—sleep? Sub plans too much trouble? I know, but sometimes you just have to bite the bullet and do it. Talk to your administrator about getting you some help. Talk to a veteran teacher who might have an out-of-the-box idea to help. Fight to retrieve the passion for your calling, don't let it go. Little lives are counting on you.

Week 15

Week 15 Day 1: Lovely Dwelling Places

"How lovely are Your dwelling places, O Lord of hosts!" Psalm 84:1

Construction paper and glue, scraps of paper snowflakes, the "Carol of the Bells" playing frantically in the background. It's Christmas! The tone of your room is festive.

"My soul yearns, even faints, for the courts of the Lord; my heart and my flesh cry out for the living God." Psalm 84:2 NIV

"It's the most wonderful time of the year," three weeks to Christmas break. You wonder how you'll keep up the pace. And why are you trying to introduce fractions?

"Blessed are those who dwell in Your house, they are ever praising you." Psalm 84:4 NIV

Dwell means to settle, and you do yearn to settle in the house of the Lord, the peace of His presence. How do you keep Christ in the midst of the festivities? How do you teach the kids to dwell in His house and not seem like a drag? Do you give up and let the season carry you away without The Reason? It's a dilemma you face every year.

Don't give up. Pray for ways to bring the Holy back into holiday. Eliminate the things that are not lovely. God's dwelling places are lovely so let's focus on the lovely. Find fresh ways to tell the Christmas story. Maybe sitting around a fake campfire with faux tea light flames. You are shepherds on the hillside. Be detectives and read the story from the Bible looking for information you never noticed before. Did Mary ride a donkey? Did the angels hover over the shepherds?

Assess your traditions. Add new ones that are lovely and eliminate ones that distract from Truth.

Do this in remembrance of me." Luke 22:19c NIV

In remembrance of Him. What a lovely place to dwell at Christmas time.

Week 15 Day 2: Magnanimous

It's a hectic day and you have a million things on your plate. Every spare moment is planned out. Then you get the call. The PE teacher is sick, no break this afternoon. You are devastated. Not only do you not get your break, but you must figure out what to do with your kids for an extra forty minutes!

Suddenly you understand how Moses felt when he came down off the mountain and found the golden calf. "Are you kidding me? I don't deserve this!"

"And he took the calf the people had made and burned it in the fire; then he ground it to powder, scattered it on the water and made the Israelites drink it." Exodus 32:20 NIV

Moses had good reason to be disappointed; his frustration was justified. So is ours. But what will be accomplished by unleashing our frustration? Most likely it will ruin our day and slop over to ruin the day of our little "Israelites." We have a split second to choose anger or grace. Being angry will not make us feel any better. We realize this is not an instance for righteous indignation. This is a time to take a deep breath and make the best of a situation that is no one's fault. It's time to be magnanimous.

Magnanimous: generous or forgiving. God is certainly magnanimous toward us. He is not only generous and forgiving, He works everything together for our good.

"And we know that God causes all things to work together for good to those who love God, to those who are called according to His purpose." Romans 8:28

How can we wring some good out of this disappointment? Maybe take our class and a neighbor's class out for some exercise so at least one of us can get a break. According to the law of sowing and reaping, this solution will eventually reap us a nice harvest when it's most needed.

"And let us not be weary in well doing; for in due season we shall reap, if we faint not." Galatians 6:9 KJV

Don't faint, be magnanimous.

Week 15 Day 3: The Note

"SEE WHAT LARGE LETTERS I USE AS I WRITE TO YOU WITH MY OWN HAND!" GALATIANS 6:11 NIV

In your pocket at the end of the day is a note. Scribbled in pencil, words misspelled, no punctuation or caps, folded awkwardly, but a treasure just the same. This note gets right to the point: "I love you," or "You are the best teacher." There may or may not be a signature, but you know who it's from. He might have perpetually dirty hands but your heart melts. You stick the note in a box or drawer to read later when you doubt you're loved or the best teacher. The praise of little ones is genuine and sincere.

"HOW PRECIOUS ARE YOUR THOUGHTS ABOUT ME, O GOD." PSALM 139:17-18 NLT

If the Lord were to write you a note, what would it say? Maybe something like: "I see you coming early and staying late to make school special for my little ones. I see the hours you spend doing the things that are necessary but not fun. I hear the cry of your heart when you don't know how to fix a situation. I see the sacrifices you make, time with your family, financial sacrifices, sanity. I see the lack of understanding and respect you deal with, my humble servant. I love you. You *are* the best teacher. I'm so proud of you my child."

"CLEARLY, YOU ARE A LETTER FROM CHRIST SHOWING THE RESULT OF OUR MINISTRY AMONG YOU. THIS "LETTER" IS WRITTEN NOT WITH PEN AND INK, BUT WITH THE SPIRIT OF THE LIVING GOD. IT IS CARVED NOT ON TABLETS OF STONE, BUT ON HUMAN HEARTS." 2 CORINTHIANS 3:3 NLT

Your little notes are treasures, but you are a treasured note yourself. A note carved on the hearts of your students, their families, and your coworkers. Not written with ink which fades or washes away, but carved, carved to last a lifetime. To last an eternity.

Week 15 Day 4: Cause and Effect

I heard a pastor the other day talking about how our prayers effect the area around us; not just the person we are praying for and not just the immediate atmosphere around us. God's presence is not like a laser that is aimed narrowly just at the need, X marks the spot. It's more like a blanket that spreads out over a large area. Have you ever stood by a campfire on a cold autumn night? Only the part of you closest to the fire is toasty warm. God's response to prayer is not like a campfire. It covers and surrounds. We often refer to the presence of the Holy Spirit as an outpouring, wide spreading.

"AS THE MOUNTAINS SURROUND JERUSALEM, SO THE LORD SURROUNDS HIS PEOPLE." PSALM 125:2

When you pray in your classroom, God's presence comes pouring out. In Malachi, God says if we tithe, He will open the windows of heaven and *pour* out a blessing until it overflows. We know *pouring* and *overflowing* and *surrounding* are actions God takes. Our prayers usher in God's presence, then His Presence spreads out and flows over our classroom and campus.

Our prayer is the *cause*; the thing that moves God. *The effect* is wide spreading. God responds to our specific need and His presence overflows next door where our neighbor teacher suddenly finds inspiration that improves a lesson, or across the hall where a struggling student finds understanding.

"HE OPENED THE ROCK, AND WATER GUSHED OUT; IT FLOWED LIKE A RIVER IN THE DESERT." PSALM 105:41 NIV

When God supplied water from a rock for His people, it wasn't a drip system trickling to fill their pots. It flowed out like a river. It benefited the desert, its creatures, and any people who happened along. It wasn't a trickle but a flood. A flood that runs through you.

"WHOEVER BELIEVES IN ME … RIVERS OF LIVING WATER WILL FLOW FROM WITHIN THEM." JOHN 7:38 NIV

Your prayer is the *cause*, and the *effect* is abundantly more than you can imagine; a flood of living water flowing through your campus.

Week 15 Day 5: Restored

"He restores my soul; He guides me in the paths of righteousness." Psalm 23:3

Let's face it, there are seasons in a school year when we need restoring. Maybe we haven't felt well, and we've been doing our least instead of our best. Perhaps we are dealing with a lot of stress in our personal life and we don't have the energy or inspiration we'd like to have. It could even be one of the kids who has nearly worn us down. As a result, we find ourselves going through the motions instead of actually teaching, plodding instead of running the good race. We need our soul restored.

"Let us not lose heart in doing good, for in due time we will reap if we do not grow weary." Galatians 6:9

I have an antique cupboard I've had since I was 12. Originally it was stained dark oak, but over the years I painted it color after color of the latest fad. Eventually my Mom decided to restore the old commode. She scraped all the layers of paint and sanded it down to the bare wood—the essence of its soul. She stained it a natural stain and coated it with polyurethane. It's a beautiful piece of furniture. It's been restored.

God is in the restoration business. Notice our verb in Psalm 23 is present tense, *restores*. God didn't only restore our soul at salvation. He restores us, now, when we feel scarred, ugly, and worn out. He sands the bumps and fills the dents. He shines and polishes until we are fresh and new again. As we take His easy yoke, we find our lost energy. Suddenly we have an idea to help Cindy Sue improve her reading. The two-ton weight we've carried around lifts off our shoulders. Sufficient grace is extended, strengthening joy surfaces.

"Your youth is renewed like the eagle's." Psalm 103:5b NIV

Week 16

 # Week 16 Day 1: Room Tone

"THE BOUNDARY LINES HAVE FALLEN FOR ME IN PLEASANT PLACES."
PSALM 16:6A NIV

God has drawn boundary lines in your life. When He established the plans for your hope and future, He set boundaries in place. Think of the pleasant places in your life. The sunny front porch of your childhood home, a farm, a beach. These places are within the boundaries God set for you.

Your student's boundaries include your classroom. You want it to be a pleasant place. As they think back on their school days you want them to remember sunny days. When I think of the room I spent the first half of third grade in, I think of sunshine. I remember a sense of belonging, feeling comfortable and capable. We moved to a different state for the second half of third grade. My memories of that room are covered in a dark cloud. I was an outsider, behind, and very uncomfortable. In retrospect I think the teacher was not happy to have another student added to her full classroom. She made no attempt to make me feel welcome.

Your kiddos are stuck in the boundaries of your classroom. They have no choice. It's up to you to make it a pleasant place. It's up to you to make each one feel welcome and accepted beginning at the door. Even when you've rushed around getting ready and didn't get your morning caffeine, you greet them with a smile because this day is not about you, it's about them. It's about showing them God has laid pleasant boundaries for them. Your room is a refuge for the girl whose mom just moved out. It's a sanctuary for the boy whose parents are doing drugs. It's a comfort for the one who lost his dog. You pat them on the head, notice their new shoes, admire their yoyo skills, and listen to their knock knock jokes. Why? Because you are making pleasant places, for yourself right along with the kids. The boundary lines have fallen in pleasant places for you all.

Week 16 Day 2: Provision

"Those who are taught the word of God should provide for their teachers, sharing all good things with them." Galatians 6:6 NLT

Yes! A specific word for the provision of Christian teachers! But it's not a popular verse, and it's not a promise but an instruction to the church. What do we do when those who are instructed to provide for us are unaware? We ask the Lord to instruct them. Does that seem selfish? It shouldn't. God will provide all our needs according to his riches in glory. We just need to ask for the release of what God already wants to do.

One year the school and church were tightening their belts so we had to go over their heads. We prayed! We asked the Lord to pour out blessings that would be more than we could contain. Soon parents became aware of the situation. A group stepped up to make sure we had what we needed in our classrooms. That same year my mom passed away. I had expenses I hadn't budgeted for. I would find envelopes of cash on my desk. It was the same for the other teachers. God spoke and moved in hearts to meet our needs. As Christian schoolteachers we work in the spiritual realm where it's God's economy that counts. We know God wants us provided for. And we know He is able.

"For I know whom I have believed and I am convinced that He is able to guard what I have entrusted to Him until that day." 2 Timothy 1:12

We commit our needs to God and trust Him to meet them. This Christmas as we face extra expenses, let's go straight to the source. Ask God to faithfully and lavishly meet our needs. Then watch what He does.

"He is the faithful God who keeps his covenant for a thousand generations and lavishes his unfailing love on those who love him and obey his commands." Deuteronomy 7:9 NLT

He will defend His Word. He is able.

Week 16 Day 3: Fill Your Lamp

One of the characters in Jan Karon's Mitford series said, "You can't shine if you don't fill your lamp." Isn't that the truth! It's a couple weeks to Christmas and your lamp is running low.

"THE FOOLISH ONES (VIRGINS) SAID TO THE WISE, "GIVE US SOME OF YOUR OIL; OUR LAMPS ARE GOING OUT." MATTHEW 25: 8 NIV

It's our responsibility to keep our lamp full. The oil for our lamp comes from time with God. If only it were as easy as plugging in our cell phone. Oh wait, it is! The hard part is finding the time to plug in. Even a few minutes in His presence helps.

"LET US NOT BECOME WEARY IN DOING GOOD, FOR AT THE PROPER TIME WE WILL REAP A HARVEST IF WE DO NOT GIVE UP." GALATIANS 6:9 NIV

Let's look at what robs our oil. Weariness drains us. Is there any way we can get a little extra rest? Can we adjust our schedule to give us some refreshing sleep?

Doing good drains us. Yes. It's good to do good but too much good and we are not much good. Is there anything we can eliminate from our schedule?

Unhealthy eating drains us. The box of chocolates on our desk, the Christmas cookies in the lounge, the fast food we grab on the run, they fill our bellies and drain our energy. Grab a clump of broccoli or a carrot for Pete's sake.

Filling our lamps during this busy season is not always convenient but it is crucial. If you're on a long road trip and you don't stop for gas now and then, what will happen? You'll run out of gas. You are on the home stretch to Christmas break.

Don't run out of gas.

Week 16 Day 4: Banana Bread

Wiping the counter down after my daughter-in-law's amazing 5 star meal, I picked up some black bananas and started toward the waste basket. Everyone gasped, "No! Don't throw them out!" It seems these bananas were being groomed for banana bread.

In a first grade class the other day I pulled out a "black banana," drop the hanky—an old game, but I gave it a phonics twist. I made banana bread. Which of your yearly lessons has become stale? What old black bananas can you add sugar to, making something old new again?

"I WILL REFRESH THE WEARY AND SATISFY THE FAINT." JEREMIAH 31:25 NIV

Is there a lesson you've taught that has become, dare I say it, boring? Don't let those black bananas lay around until they're mush, now is the time for banana bread. For example, there's a chapter in our history book about The Great Awakening. It highlights the men who led the movement. It's a pretty boring read but I've never skipped it because I want the kids to know these great men of faith. I asked myself, were the kids learning anything by reading this chapter? I had to admit, no. I prayed about it and made banana bread. We did a jigsaw activity. I divided the kids into groups and assigned a famous man of faith to each group. They had to read a section in the History book and do a project on it. They could make a poster, a collage, or write a skit. After a couple days of work, they all presented their projects. While one group presented, the spectators filled out graphic organizers from the information they gleaned. Did the project take longer than reading the chapter? Yes. Was it more trouble for me? Yes. Did they learn more than they would have? Yes! Was it boring? No! It was banana bread.

Jigsawing is an old teacher trick. The chapter on The Great Awakening was boring. Two black bananas together with some sugar and eggs made something old new again. Don't be afraid to hang on to something old and make it fresh.

Week 16 Day 5: The Big Question

"AND HE (PAUL) TREMBLING AND ASTONISHED SAID, "LORD, WHAT WILL YOU HAVE ME TO DO?" ACTS 9:6 KJV

Teachers make so many decisions a day and often those decisions must be made with no prior experience to help us. Right at the onset Paul asks God, "What will you have me to do?" His words are words of surrender, a free offer with no strings attached. "What do you want of me, God?" No agenda. Just simple, sincere, and slightly desperate surrender. JFK said, "Ask not what your country can do for you, ask what you can do for your country." Paul asks what can he do for his God.

"THEN I HEARD THE VOICE OF THE LORD SAYING, 'WHOM SHALL I SEND? AND WHO WILL GO FOR US?' AND I SAID, 'HERE AM I. SEND ME!'" ISAIAH 6:8 NIV

This big question is, "What will You do through me, Lord? I'm tired of trying to do it on my own strength. I give up the reins to you."

There are three fifth grade boys at my school who pop their heads in my room every night to see if I need any help. They are up for anything, moving furniture, running errands, or cleaning. What if we started our day that way? "Lord, I'm at your disposal, what would you have me to do today? I take your yoke upon me." Imagine the doors that might open! Imagine the opportunities that might arise! Imagine stepping out from the stress of the thousand decisions we make each day and just trusting God! Oh, the benefits of surrender, the refreshing rest, the peace that passes understanding.

What if we just commit our day to Him; expecting Him to lead us beside still waters, trusting Him to give us a right spirit? Surrendering stress and self?

"Lord, what will you have me to do?"

Week 17

Week 17 Day 1: It's Not Fair

"It's not fair," is a phrase we hear often from students. They are like vultures circling the sky looking for discrepancies. "Benny only had to do five of the ten math problems." "Lulu gets to stay in at recess for help when everyone else has to go out." "Jimmy gets to use a fat pencil and sit on a big ball." It's tough to explain to the kiddos that very little is fair in this world. Who introduced the concept that everything had to be fair anyway?

"I WILL GIVE THANKS TO YOU, FOR I AM FEARFULLY AND WONDERFULLY MADE." PSALM 139:14

We are each made uniquely special for the life God has planned for us. That's fair. The idea of something being not fair comes from comparison. Is it fair that Joey can run faster than Jimmy? Not to a first grader. First graders don't understand that we are all given diverse gifts fairly in order to fulfill God's plans for us.

Is it fair the teacher next door is smarter? Is it fair another is gifted at using music with her teaching, or another can mesmerize her students with dramatic flair? What about the one who is contagious about geography? Yes, it's fair. It's fair that each of us add something to enrich a child's life in different ways.

"FOR IT IS GOD WHO IS AT WORK IN YOU, BOTH TO WILL AND TO WORK FOR HIS GOOD PLEASURE." PHILIPPIANS 2:13

Just as you treat your kiddos fairly by making accommodations for them to succeed, God works in you uniquely to accomplish His will. You are equipped to connect with the little guy who didn't relate to the dramatic, musical, geography loving teachers who preceded you. Or maybe you *are* dramatic and musical. Whichever, you are just what he needs. It's his turning-point year because you are wonderfully and fearfully made to make a difference in lives this year. Yes, it *is* fair.

Week 17 Day 2: Stir Up

This close to Christmas the last thing you want to do is stir things up. Your class is already stirred up enough. But if we are going to survive till break, we need our spirit to rally.

"THEREFORE I REMIND YOU TO STIR UP THE GIFT OF GOD WHICH IS IN YOU." 2 TIMOTHY 1:6 NKJV

When I was in 4th grade we lived in a house with a primitive coal furnace. Dad loaded it with coal at bedtime but by morning it was nearly out. There was a pan Dad would shake so the ash would fall below the firebox. If he was lucky there might be some embers left to start a new fire for the day. Unless the fire was tended, it went out.

The *stirring up* our verse refers to is similar. It's like bringing life to dying embers. We are embers. We begin as a shiny lump of coal, full of potential. At morning recess, we burn brightly but by lunch we are fading. We continue burning through the end of the school day and hopefully have a little spark for our family in the evening. By the time we hit the bed we are pretty much ash. Like Dad's fire, we need tending. We cry out for the Lord to stir us, to shake down the ash and renew the flame of His fire in us.

As I read our verse from 2 Timothy, I wondered, "How do we stir up the gift of God?" The Gift is the Holy Spirit. How can we stir up the Holy Spirit? I think we do what my dad did, we shake down the ash. We brush away the effects of the world so the God ember can burn.

"AND WITH THAT HE BREATHED ON THEM AND SAID, "RECEIVE THE HOLY SPIRIT." JOHN 20:22 NIV

We allow the Lord to breathe fresh on us. The Spirit flames up and once again we are a shiny lump of coal able to warm and illuminate another day in the lives of our students and loved ones.

Tend your fire.

Week 17 Day 3: Held

"When I thought, "My foot slips," your steadfast love, O Lord, held me up." Psalm 94:18 ESV

Let's look at the Hebrew definition of *held*: to yoke or hitch; to join battle, gird, keep, make ready, and to prepare. Wow! Seriously, look that over again. We all need to be held, don't we?

Are there days when you feel abandoned and alone in a classroom full of kids? I think we all feel that way now and then. Maybe there are troubles at home or it's a particularly difficult class or we are overwhelmed, or a million other reasons. We must remember, feelings are sometimes liars.

One fall, my students brought in a chrysalis on a stick. We put it in a jar and waited. I thought we'd have *something* in a month or two. Nothing. By Christmas it was looking bad. I was sure it was dead and wanted to throw it out. The kids begged me not to. By the end of the school year it still hadn't emerged, but in true Scarlett O'Hara form I decided to deal with it later. In July when I came to prepare for the next school year, there, in the jar, was a huge swallowtail butterfly! My intellect said it was dead. But that butterfly was held, and he emerged to be so beautiful. He looked a little frail though. I took him on my finger to the back door. I wondered if he'd be able to fly. He sat on my finger long enough that I was about to give up but then, off he went! He was strong! He was held safely until he could fly.

When we feel like a dead chrysalis hanging on a stick by a thread, we are actually being held. When we feel abandoned and alone, it's a lie.

"Your steadfast love, O Lord, held me up." Psalm 94:18b ESV

Picture the scene in Lion King where Rafiki holds Simba up. God holds us up. Up above the turmoil of the earth, of our class, of our home.

We are held and held high.

Week 17 Day 4: Remainders

"So too, at the present time there is a remnant chosen by grace."
Romans 11:5 NIV

You must admire the little remainder in a division problem. He was there from the beginning, living with the dividend in their little house. Then along comes the Divisor and the process begins. One thing after another, all meant to rip them apart. The whole purpose of Divisor is to bring division! The little remainder tries to stand for truth but time and time again he gets knocked down. In the end he stands alone. A bold declaration of his value. The world would be less without him—but even more, it would be wrong.

The fact is, we are remainders. We are Esthers, remnants chosen for such a time as this. We can expect to face the Divisor often in our school year. His purpose is division where God wants unity. Often, I'm asked, "Do these problems have remainders?" When I answer, "Yes," the kids are disappointed. They don't like remainders, and yet we are training them to *be* remainders. We want them to stand strong and stand alone, if necessary. We are educating a generation of remainders!

"How good and pleasant it is when God's people live together in unity!"
Psalm 133:1 NIV

It's interesting to read the list of the "works of the flesh" in Galatians 5: immorality, impurity, idolatry, etc. Right there, among all the terrible things, are discord and factions! It gives us a good idea how God feels about disunity. As remainders training remainders we must be alert and not fall for the wiles of the devil. We must not be tricked into disunity by the Accuser of the Brethren or any forces of darkness. We must teach our students to be wise to Satan's tricks.

It's my desire, and I'm sure yours too, for my class to be a team; working together, supporting each other. A team needs a common goal. As a team of remainders our common goal is love. The process to rid our lives of disunity is to love. Love births unity.

Stand tall, love unconditionally, and REMAIN.

Week 17 Day 5: Survivor

It's the last sane Friday before break. All you can hope to accomplish next week is to survive. You're probably taking your last grades and hoping the kids haven't quit trying yet.

Did you see the original season of the show, Survivor? People were dumped off a boat near an island and had to survive by their wits, skills, and whatever they could find on the island. That pretty much describes the upcoming week. What wits and skills do you have that will organize the chaos of the "Island of the Week Before Christmas?" This island is like Tahiti except it's cold and the natives are hostile.

"SEE, I HAVE CHOSEN BEZALEL AND FILLED HIM WITH THE SPIRIT OF GOD, WITH WISDOM, UNDERSTANDING, KNOWLEDGE, AND ALL KINDS OF SKILLS—TO MAKE ARTISTIC DESIGNS, AND TO ENGAGE IN ALL KINDS OF CRAFTS."
EXODUS 31:2–5 PWV (PEGGY WHITE VERSION)

Your enemy next week is boredom. Nothing can be boring. We need 100% engagement 100% of the time. Oh wait, that's always our goal. It just takes more effort now. Oh Lord, we need a Bezalel anointing!

Let's look at Bezalel's situation. First off, he was chosen by God. Hey, so are you. Second, he was filled with the Holy Spirit. So are you. Third, God filled Bezalel with wisdom and understanding. You have the mind of Christ, so you're good.

"AND HE HAS GIVEN BOTH HIM (BEZALEL) AND OHOLIAB ... THE ABILITY TO TEACH OTHERS." EXODUS 35:34 NIV

Fourth, God gave Bezalel helpers. Get yourself some help next week. Are there parents or grandparents who could come in and help? Don't try to do games and intricate crafts by yourself. Remember, your goal is survival and sanity.

"THEY RECEIVED FROM MOSES ALL THE OFFERING THE ISRAELITES HAD BROUGHT TO CARRY OUT THE WORK." EXODUS 36:3 NIV

Fifth, Moses asked the people to pitch in. Usually parents will respond to a request for supplies. Don't take the expense on yourself. Make specific requests: Barney family, can you bring pickles? Finally, God gave Bezalel a special ability to teach others. You have that too.

You are a survivor!

Week 18

Week 18
Day 1

I will be honest. I debated about skipping week 18, the week before Christmas break, because I doubt you'll have the time or inclination for a devotion. But I decided to offer some practical suggestions for those of you who haven't taught thirty some years. I am going to throw out some suggestions and you are welcome to try them or ignore them.

1. I pace the Christmas story so I get to the part about the shepherds on Monday or Tuesday of this week. I mentioned earlier making a campfire of river rocks and battery tea lights (Week 15, Day 1). In the center I place one short fat candle with three wicks, one that won't easily tip. I have the classroom lights out and my campfire on when the kids come in. I have them sit quietly around the "fire" and I tell the story. I like to stress what it must have been like for the shepherds; never having seen anything very amazing, no movies or tv, no concerts, not even electric lights. Then, bam! Suddenly a big glowy man appears. We talk about how shocking that must have been. Ok, now I'm getting to the part you will think is crazy. I let two kids (4th grade) at a time roast a marshmallow over the one real candle. I pull them off the stick so no one gets burned. I've done this for many years and never had any problems. While they take turns roasting, we sing Christmas carols. It's always been a special, memorable time and puts some new life in the story they've heard many times.

2. Today is probably a good time to start the dreaded Christmas present for Mom. Years ago, I found one I love so I'll pass it on. We make dangly earrings for Mom. Dad's present is getting to see Mom look so pretty. Moms who don't have pierced ears can give them to someone else who does have pierced ears. Generally, everyone loves them, and the kids love making them. All you need are: some long pin-like things that look like long straight pins, earring wires that go through Mom's ears, lots of small beads, and a plier-like tool that bends and cuts. You can watch YouTube videos on how to make these. Search "How to make beaded dangle earrings." Super easy. Probably second grade and up can do these with you doing the wire bending and cutting. Later this week you can make gift wrap envelopes for your earrings.

Week 18
Day 2

Continuing today with some practical (or not so practical) ideas of things to do this week, the last week of the semester.

1. Finish up the Christmas story today. It's probably the last day they will sit and listen to a story. I use the campfire again, then have them help me dismantle it and put the rocks and candles where they belong.

2. For Math this week I always do a lot of flashcard games, math bingo, and competitions. I have collected a few Monopoly games and I like to ask kids to bring in some more so we can have Monopoly Day. I would not try this for under 4th grade. Monopoly Day is actually Monopoly hour. I have it down to a science. First, you need an adult for every board. Have the kids pass out the money. You post the amounts on the board. One kid can pass out the $500s and $100s, another can pass out the $50s and $20s, and so on. The adult should shuffle and pass out all the property cards just like you'd pass out a deck of cards. You get what you get and you don't throw a fit. Some kids might end up with one less card than others. This way the kids can begin trading for monopolies right away. They have to figure out all the money stuff and ask the banker (adult) for the bills they need or give the amount they owe. That's where the math comes in. The game ends in an hour. Whoever has the most houses and hotels is the winner.

3. Many of us go caroling to missions and nursing homes. A few years ago, I had the idea to also carol for the office staff of the school and church. It's nice and you don't even need a field trip permission slip.

4. Snowflakes. I'll admit I hate making snowflakes, all those tiny scraps all over the floor, and I'm not even a neat freak! But I bite the bullet and help them make snowflakes during the week before Christmas. If you have younger kids maybe you can borrow a few big kids to help. If you want, you can give the snowflakes to the office staff when you carol. Two birds.

Week 18
Day 3

1. Writing. One of my all-time favorite projects is making a story walk. I stole this idea from the public library in Sedona, Arizona. As a class we made up a story about Mary and Joseph's trip from Nazareth to Bethlehem told from the perspective of the donkey. We brainstormed what they might see and what might happen along the way. They even saw dinosaurs! We named the donkey and started our first page with Mary getting on board. We ended with the nativity scene. Each child chose something from our brainstorming and made a first draft of a picture with a few sentences at the bottom like a page from a picture book. I did some editing and added a few words to tie the pages together like a continuous story. Then I gave the kids some cardstock to make a nice picture and copy their revised sentences on. They really took pride in making and coloring nice pictures. The artists in the class helped those who struggle with drawing and those with great printing helped others too. I numbered and laminated the pages then we mixed them up and tied them to the preschool fence. We arranged a time with the preschool teacher to take them on our story walk. My kids helped the littles hunt for each page in numerical order and then read the page to them, continuing till the story was complete. We served them hot chocolate too. We all loved it. We made the book one day and did the story walk another day.

2. By the middle of the week it's hard to get them to listen to a Bible lesson so I like to play a competitive game like sword drills, Bible trivia, or the name game. If you don't have a sword drill book, you can use the concordance of your bible to look up a subject like *love* and use the references you find there. For Bible trivia you might want to make up your own questions over the lessons you've had so far this year. I sometimes divided the class into two teams and used the trivia questions to play tic tac toe on the board. Each team had to answer a question right to earn their X or O.

The name game is something I made up years ago but is a lot like Headbands. You call a student up front and have them face the class while you write the name of a Bible character on the board. Then they call on kids to give them hints about who they are. This game is great for history and science terms too.

Week 18
Day 4

You've almost made it! The finish line is in view.

1. If you haven't pulled out the Math bingo yet, today is the day to do it.

2. In my class we are usually on geometry at Christmas so a favorite game is geometry charades. I made little cards with geometry terms and the kids pick a card, act it out, and call on people to guess what they are. They can choose partners for things like parallel and triangle. It's fun and they are very creative.

3. This might also be a good day for an in-school snow day. Everyone wears jammies and brings in a favorite book, board game, or Legos. Pillows, stuffed animals, and blankets are also welcome.

4. Even if you have older kids, Show-and-Tell is a nice option today. Maybe ask for a specific show-and-tell, like a favorite (unbreakable) ornament.

5. Similar to in-school snow day is Library sleepover. If the library is available and the librarian doesn't mind and your kids are old enough to put books back where they belong, a Library sleepover is a lot of fun. It's not really a sleepover, you just get to wear jammies. I take them to the library with flashlights. I have a bunch of flashlights for Science but you could ask them to bring them from home. One flashlight per two or three kids is enough. I have them go to the picture book section and with a buddy or two, read by flashlight some of the old picture books they love. This doesn't work as well if you have a bright sunny library. I let them sit under the table too—always popular.

6. Today is a great day to clean out desks so they will be clean and tidy after break. Have them take home all the toys and do-dads they have unlawfully accumulated and make the desks look like they did on the first day of school. Send home a note, text, email, and Facebook appeal requesting new school supplies to replace the ones that are worn out or missing.

Week 18 Day 5: You Made It!

You made it! Only a few more hours and you're on break! All you have to do is get through Party Day. Hopefully it's a half day. If it's not a half day, hopefully you can show a movie!

1. Pace your day wisely. Whether you have a half day or a full day, don't start the party too soon and run out of things to do before dismissal. Today, no matter how old your kids are, you are herding kittens. If you lose control of your kittens, you will never get them back. You want to have fun but not too much fun!
2. Start your day with some semblance of normalcy. They will want to jump right into party mode. Don't let them. Today's games should start out tame. Maybe a spelling bee of Christmas words
3. or words from the lists they've completed. They might seem disappointed at first. Remember, they came to school expecting dancing and food fights, presents and revelry. Settle them down before you stir them up. Do whole group activities. Cooperative learning groups today would be cooperative chaos groups.
4. Play Show Me. You ask a Christmas trivia question, they write the answer on their little white boards, you say "Show me," they show, and get a tally mark in the corner of their board if they are right. Everyone who gets a certain number right can take off their shoes or sit on their desk or sing a fun song or something that is a treat to them.
5. When it's time for the party to start, I like to do the food first. I assign certain things to certain people. You know who can afford what and who you can count on. I always ask for just one sweet treat: birthday cupcakes for Jesus' birthday. We set a special time to nicely sing Happy birthday to Jesus. For older kids I would take a moment to have them pray and thank Jesus. The rest of the treats are non-sweet, although someone usually surprises me with cookies and candy galore. We set up a junk food buffet and fill our plates so they can snack during the next part of the party.
6. Presents. I'm going to tell you a terrible secret about me. Some teachers don't do gift exchanges anymore for various unselfish reasons. I still do a gift exchange because it's a great time filler on party day! I draw sticks for kids to come up one at a time to open their gift and ooh and ah over it, and politely thank the one who gave it. Before we open, I always give a little lecture about properly thanking the person even if you already have whatever you got or even if you hate it.
7. If you timed your day right, you should have time for one short game and out the door they go!

Week 19

Week 19 Day 1: Settled

"THEN, WHAT LOOKED LIKE FLAMES OR TONGUES OF FIRE APPEARED AND SETTLED ON EACH OF THEM." ACTS 2:3 NLT

The other day I watched a duck settle down for the night. He circled around a few times, drew his feet up under himself, lifted a wing a bit, turned his head to his wing, and tucked himself in. He was settled. Similarly, the Holy Spirit is settled in you. He is tucked in and comfortable with you. He knows your ways and needs. He offers the warmth and steady flame for day to day life, but He will also blaze into powerful flames when you need it.

"THE SPIRIT OF THE SOVEREIGN LORD IS UPON ME, FOR THE LORD HAS ANOINTED ME TO BRING GOOD NEWS TO THE POOR." ISAIAH 61:1 NLT

As you begin the second half of your school year, you are not alone. The Holy Spirit is settled in you. You begin this new semester fully equipped and anointed. Last night you prayed for one more day of Christmas break; you needed just one more day. You didn't feel at all ready to go back. But here you are today, up at the crack of dawn, heading back to school. Ready or not. You *are* ready though, whether you feel it or not, you have the Divine edge: "Christ in you, the hope of glory." The Holy Spirit doesn't need one more day. As you ease back into the yoke of school, He is with you. When your sleepy heads enter the classroom, His love will well up inside you. When you open your mouth for the Bible lesson, He will speak through you. As you introduce that new math concept, sudden inspiration will spring up. You are back in the groove—settled.

It's going to be a great quarter. Not only are *you* settled, but so are the kiddos. You are entering a season of great growth. The kids know what you require from them and you know what they are capable of. So much is accomplished in this nine-week period. Along with the kids and the Holy Spirit, you are settled.

In it for the long haul.

Week 19 Day 2: Lightbulb!

"It's the most wonderful time of the year!" Many believe Christmas is the most wonderful time of the year, but teachers know it's the third quarter. It is then the lightbulbs come on.

"I WILL SEND YOU RAIN IN ITS SEASON, AND THE GROUND WILL YIELD ITS CROPS AND THE TREES THEIR FRUIT." LEVITICUS 26:4 NIV

Third quarter is the season when all the rain you've poured out begins to produce a crop. Your little plunkers begin to catch on. For some reason it seems the kiddos are more focused and attentive this quarter than any of the others. There's nothing better than seeing the look of understanding on the face of a struggler. They begin to relate their school learning to everyday life! Ronnie can read the lunchroom sign; Lucy can count change. Now you remember why you do what you do. Oh, the joy when Sofie "gets it!" If you had a football, you'd throw it down and do a touchdown dance. All year you've encouraged yourself, "They'll get it. The Lord will help." And now you begin to see your words of life pay off.

"BY FAITH WE UNDERSTAND THAT THE UNIVERSE WAS FORMED AT GOD'S COMMAND, SO THAT WHAT IS SEEN WAS NOT MADE OUT OF WHAT WAS VISIBLE." HEBREWS 11:3 NIV

A lot of faith is needed in teaching—trusting things are going on in the unseen realm. The planting and watering you've been doing all year effects the unseen realm. Things are happening in little hearts and minds, invisible things. Like bulbs in the warm spring soil, roots are going down, hidden sprouts are ready to uncurl. On the surface there is no evidence but in the unseen realm growth is occurring. Then suddenly, or so it seems, what was invisible become visible. Little green leaves break through, and a bud! The lightbulb comes on.

"I PLANTED THE SEED, APOLLOS WATERED IT, BUT GOD HAS BEEN MAKING IT GROW." 1 CORINTHIANS 3:6 NIV

Week 19 Day 3: The Blessing

"THE LORD BLESS YOU, AND KEEP YOU; THE LORD MAKE HIS FACE SHINE ON YOU, AND BE GRACIOUS TO YOU; THE LORD LIFT UP HIS COUNTENANCE ON YOU, AND GIVE YOU PEACE." NUMBERS 6:24–26

God instructed Aaron to speak this over His special people, Israel. When he did, God blessed. It's cause and effect again. Cause: Aaron spoke a blessing over the people. Effect: God blessed them. What a powerful thing, to be the releaser of God's blessing!

You are the shepherd of your little flock, the priest of your classroom. You bless the kids in so many ways: planning engaging lessons, listening to their stories, praying for them, loving them. It's easy to get caught up in all that and forget to stop and speak a blessing over them.

"SO, THEY SHALL INVOKE MY NAME ON THE SONS OF ISRAEL, AND I THEN WILL BLESS THEM." NUMBERS 6:27

You stop now and then and tell them you love them and how they make you happy. But do you ever invoke God's name over them? *You* bless them but do you call for God's blessing over them?

Your blessing is wonderful but the blessing of the Name above all names is supernatural. Your blessing is a natural blessing. You speak it and their hearts are blessed. But the blessing in the Name of the Lord is far above a blessing sourced in yourself. Its source is unlimited and eternal. A blessing spoken in the name of the Lord releases His power and plans into lives. The Living Water inside you flows out and changes the atmosphere and circumstances. You are unleashing the power and will of God Almighty. Have you ever seen someone let a very eager dog off their leash? They take off like a bullet. When you speak God's blessing over your kids, you unleash God's power. Who knows what He will do.

Unleash it!

Week 19 Day 4: Broke

It's the week after Christmas break and all that's in your pocket is a used tissue. Payday cannot come soon enough. You add a little more pasta and sauce to stretch out your family's evening meal. You pray for gas prices to go down. And speaking of down, you turn the thermostat a little below comfortable. You're broke—again.

When you're broke Satan comes to visit with his Santa-bag full of doubt. He whispers in his naggy voice, "Does God really want you to teach? You could make more money doing something else. If God wanted you here wouldn't He prosper you?" It's an old trick, going back to the Garden of Eden, but an effective one: planting seeds of doubt. Do not listen. God is good, faithful, and His love is unfailing. Unfailing. He leads you beside still waters. You will get through this. Just because you're broke doesn't mean God isn't faithful. You will go through difficulties, but the point is, you go *through*. He won't leave you in a pit or a prison.

"AND MY GOD WILL MEET ALL YOUR NEEDS ACCORDING TO THE RICHES OF HIS GLORY IN CHRIST JESUS." PHILIPPIANS 4:19 NIV

I've taught over thirty years. I've been underpaid, taken pay cuts, and gone summers without pay, but my needs were always met. Looking back, I can't think of a single time my family didn't have what we needed. Satan wants to use tight finances to make you doubt God. God wants to use the situation to display His faithfulness.

"WHEN HE HAD DISARMED THE RULERS AND AUTHORITIES HE MADE A PUBLIC DISPLAY OF THEM, HAVING TRIUMPHED OVER THEM THROUGH HIM." COLOSSIANS 2:15

The Bible tells us God leads us on a plain path. If He wants you to change vocations, He will tell you. And it won't be a naggy voice. It will be a voice of peace. When you are disturbed and confused, when you doubt, Satan is the source of it.

Go ahead and add more spaghetti to the pot tonight. Soon enough you'll be dining on steak. After all, He is Jehovah Jireh, our Provider.

Week 19 Day 5: Skipping Church

"NOT FORSAKING OUR OWN ASSEMBLING TOGETHER, AS IS THE HABIT OF SOME, BUT ENCOURAGING ONE ANOTHER; AND ALL THE MORE AS YOU SEE THE DAY DRAWING NEAR." HEBREWS 10:25

You spend all day Saturday doing the things you can't do during the week. It's not even really a day off. Then Sunday rolls round and you have church and perhaps a class Sunday afternoon and then lesson plans or grading Sunday night. Day of rest? That's a laugh. There is no day of rest during the school year. Skipping church is a real temptation. It's also very dangerous. As our verse says, skipping church can become a habit. You need church and church needs you. At church you find medicine for your soul and you dispense medicine to others through your Rivers of Living Water.

"THEREFORE ENCOURAGE ONE ANOTHER AND BUILD UP ONE ANOTHER, JUST AS YOU ALSO ARE DOING." 1 THESSALONIANS 5:11

Satan does not want you encouraged and built up. He whispers in your ear, "It's ok, just sleep in, you need the rest." He's probably right. It *is* ok to sleep in and rest now and then. But what do we sacrifice? We miss a timely word from our pastor, we miss God's presence in worship, we miss those things God speaks to us at church and we miss the members of our body. The danger is not in skipping church but in letting it become a habit. The more we miss, the harder it is to return. The more we miss, the weaker we become. We are an example for our students. They notice when we're not at church. We send a message not only to our students but to our own family that church is not important.

"SO THAT YOU MAY BECOME BLAMELESS AND PURE, 'CHILDREN OF GOD WITHOUT FAULT IN A WARPED AND CROOKED GENERATION.' THEN YOU WILL SHINE AMONG THEM LIKE STARS IN THE SKY." PHILIPPIANS 2:15 NIV

You are a shining star. All week you plant and water your little seedlings. Church is your opportunity to get planted and watered. Don't deny yourself the very medicine you need.

A spoonful of sugar.

Week 20

Week 20 Day 1: Withdraws

Your year is ticking along nicely when you hear a child is being withdrawn from your classroom. You are devastated. Teachers take it personally when parents remove their child from our care.

"AND THERE OCCURRED SUCH A SHARP DISAGREEMENT THAT THEY SEPARATED FROM ONE ANOTHER, AND BARNABAS TOOK MARK WITH HIM AND SAILED AWAY TO CYPRUS." ACTS 15:39

You opened your heart to this child. You aren't prepared to let him go midyear. It feels like divorce—a stab to your heart. Often in these situations the parents don't allow you and the classmates to say good-bye. You and your students are hurt, and the child is hurt. You've been a family. You've worked hard to build relationship and now a piece of your puzzle is lost, sailed away to Cyprus.

On top of this wound, you worry, "Did he get enough from our Bible lessons?" Or, "Does he have a lasting relationship with Jesus?" Remember, you are not the child's Savior. This withdraw is no surprise to God. He has a plan for the child and being removed from your classroom does not affect God's plan and faithfulness.

"I PLANTED, APOLLOS WATERED, BUT GOD WAS CAUSING THE GROWTH." 1 CORINTHIANS 3:6

Your job was to plant and water, not to crawl up on the cross. Jesus took care of that. This child's salvation is in His hands.

Talk with your class about how you feel. Give them a chance to share their feelings, especially the best friend who is more devastated than you. Pray together, pull together. Use this opportunity to demonstrate how to go through a loss with the Lord. Make sure your kiddos don't suffer with abandonment; especially the group of friends who were close to him. If possible, ask the parents to allow a going-away party to put a more positive spin on a difficult situation.

Finally, don't accept any blame or condemnation. God will work this to good as He always does.

"THEREFORE, THERE IS NOW NO CONDEMNATION FOR THOSE WHO ARE IN CHRIST JESUS." ROMANS 8:1

No condemnation.

Week 20 Day 2: Stuck

You've introduced the topic, explained, modeled, and provided manipulatives. You've worked in cooperative learning groups, done structures, and played games, but they still don't seem to be getting it. You're stuck. But there's one more tool in your toolbox: the Divine Edge.

"BE FILLED WITH THE KNOWLEDGE OF HIS WILL IN ALL SPIRITUAL WISDOM AND UNDERSTANDING." COLOSSIANS 1:9B

I've prayed this many times. When you get stuck and can't think of a way for the kids to *get* a concept, pray this verse; not just over yourself, but over them as well. There's also a partner verse I pray often when I'm stuck.

"THAT GOD … MAY GIVE TO YOU THE SPIRIT OF WISDOM AND REVELATION IN THE KNOWLEDGE OF HIM.… THAT THE EYES OF YOUR UNDERSTANDING MAY BE ENLIGHTENED." EPHESIANS 1:17–18A NKJV

Wisdom, revelation, enlightened understanding, along with the knowledge of His will? That should do the trick. It's amazing what happens when we stop and pray God's Word.

"FOR THE WORD OF GOD IS LIVING AND ACTIVE AND SHARPER THAN ANY TWO-EDGED SWORD." HEBREWS 4:12A

Isn't it funny how we run ragged leaning on our own understanding, on our own ability? We have at our disposal God's wisdom. We have the mind of Christ and ears to hear what the Spirit of the Lord is saying. All we need to do is tune in.

Old TVs and radios had a dial called a tuner. If a station was staticky you would turn the tuner slightly. The tuner would bring in the station clearly and tune out the static. Sometimes our abilities become static. We need to tune out the static of our own understanding and tune in the mind of Christ.

"TRUST IN THE LORD WITH ALL YOUR HEART AND LEAN NOT ON YOUR OWN UNDERSTANDING; IN ALL YOUR WAYS SUBMIT TO HIM, AND HE WILL MAKE YOUR PATHS STRAIGHT." PROVERBS 3:5-6 NIV

Once we get our own understanding out of the way we can take His straight path—unstuck.

Week 20 Day 3:
A Message

"I have a message from God in my heart." Psalm 36:1a NIV

Do you have a message from God in your heart? You should share it with your kiddos. They love to hear testimonies. You can tell them all about Moses or David, or even George Washington, but that's secondhand knowledge, a secondary source. When you tell them about God's faithfulness firsthand, they listen. Your personal stories are the ones they take home and share with their families.

"And they overcame him because of the blood of the Lamb and because of the word of their testimony." Revelation 12:11

You have a message that could stick with them their whole life. How did you get saved? What miracles has God done in your life? What verses has God given you and how did they apply in your life? Look for opportunities to share these, even if it comes to you in the middle of math class. What blessed freedom we have to share our testimonies. If the Holy Spirit reminds you of something during math, He has a reason. Maybe God supplied food when you were out of money. God does stuff like that all the time. The kids need to hear it and their families need to hear the message of God's unfailing love.

What about your kiddos? Do they have a message? Give them opportunities to share. Teach them to pray for each other so they can see God answer their prayers. One of my first years of teaching I decided to write our everyday prayer requests on a poster so we could check them off when God answered. Over Christmas break, being a person of great faith, I subtly hid the poster because none of our prayers seemed to be answered. Near the end of the year I ran on to the poster and, surprise surprise, everything on the poster had been answered! What a testimony it was to the kids—and me!

Week 20 Day 4: Heartily

"And whatsoever you do, do it heartily as to the Lord, and not unto men." Colossians 3:23 KJV

We are to do whatever we do heartily, like we would if the Lord were standing right beside us. Most days we feel pretty good if we reach the heights of *okay*. But heartily, with gusto? At this point we are just trying to survive to Martin Luther King Day. Does the Lord really expect gusto when we get up in the dark, teach all day, and go home in the dark? There don't seem to be any qualifiers.

I'm a big Disneyland fan and when I think of someone working heartily, I think of cast members at Disney. They don't just do their jobs, they go beyond. They become part of the magic of Disneyland. They are always pleasant, helpful, and enthusiastic, even when they're busy, even in the middle of winter. And isn't that what we want for ourselves and our kids, to go beyond mediocre? Our heart's desire is to teach with gusto so it's time to stir things up.

"Therefore I remind you to stir up the gift of God which is in you." 2 Timothy 1:6 NKJV

What can you do to get your gusto back? Is there a conference you can attend? What about taking a personal day? Go to a movie, get a pedicure. Are you thinking, "Too expensive," or "Too much trouble?" Think of it as an investment. You need refreshing. You are worth it. You deserve to be renewed. Ask God to help. He made quite an investment in you already, He *wants* to restore your gusto. And He will treat you with gusto, heartily.

"For out of Jerusalem will go forth a remnant, and out of Mount Zion survivors. The zeal of the Lord will perform this." 2 Kings 19:31

Zeal equals hearty and with gusto. May His zeal be contagious to you.

Week 20 Day 5: Sick

"'I cannot go to school today,' Said little Peggy Ann McKay." Or more appropriately, said Shel Silverstein in his poem, "Sick." It's one of my favorite poems.

You woke up not feeling well, you're trying to decide if you can make it through the day or if you should get a sub. Going in sick is easier than getting ready for a sub. Urgh. Stop and think for a minute. Have you been exposed to anything? Did you eat something that upset your tummy? If you can't pin down a reason for feeling so lousy, maybe you aren't sick at all, maybe it's a spirit of infirmity.

"And, behold, there was a woman which had a spirit of infirmity eighteen years." Luke 13:11 KJV

You are certainly exposed to all kinds of germs at school but there are times when you have oddball symptoms that could be demonic. Your throat feels tight, your heart is pounding, or, like Peggy Ann McKay, you have "A gash, a rash and purple bumps." They could be legitimate problems, or they could be caused by a spirit of infirmity.

To battle infirmity, speak out any scriptures on healing that come to mind. Ephesians 4:25 tells us to put off falsehood so I say out loud, "I put off any spirit of affliction or infirmity in the name of Jesus. My body is the temple of the Holy Spirit." As I say this, I put my hands in front of me and push them forward like I was pushing a heavy door. I *put off* anything that is out of God's will and I say the Name of Jesus above it.

"Therefore God exalted him to the highest place and gave him the name that is above every name." Philippians 2:9 NIV

After you pray and put off, go ahead and start getting ready for school. Often, you will feel better before you get to school. Don't give into symptoms without doing some spiritual warfare first. God is on your team.

Week 21

Week 21 Day 1: Full-Time

At home your family is stressful: sick kids, finances, unsaved loved ones, whatever. At school life is stressful: observation coming up, Billy and Willie are fighting again, no one is getting area and perimeter. There isn't a moment in your day when there's nothing to worry about. You are a full-time worrier.

"AND WHICH OF YOU BY BEING OVERLY ANXIOUS *AND* TROUBLED WITH CARES CAN ADD A CUBIT TO HIS STATURE *OR* A MOMENT [UNIT] OF TIME TO HIS AGE [THE LENGTH OF HIS LIFE]?" LUKE 12:25 AMPC

You *know* worrying does no good, but you have very legitimate reasons to worry and you feel guilty and irresponsible if you don't. Our verse says it so well, you have *cares*, you care so very much. You are a professional at caring—full-time.

Recently a missionary friend posted on social media a statement that caught my attention. God is a full-time God. He compared it to alcohol which is a part-time solution. Alcohol helps for a while; temporary relief. God is not a temporary fix; He's not a part-timer or a sub or temp. He never sleeps or slumbers.

"AND LO, I AM WITH YOU ALWAYS, EVEN TO THE END OF THE AGE." MATTHEW 28:20B

He is *with* you, He will never leave you or forsake you. And your worries? He will never forsake them either. Your worry only feeds your fear. The more you worry, the bigger your fear becomes. Focusing on worries distracts you from the facts of God's ability, goodness, and faithfulness. Yes, you have legitimate reasons to worry but you can choose to turn them over to God. Then they become trust.

The Bible says God will supply all our needs (full-time) according to His riches in glory. God has your worries covered. He has plans to take care of them, working all things together for good. Your classroom observation? God's with you, He makes His face shine upon you. God never takes a break, not even recess. He is on duty 24/7 and nothing is impossible for him.

"CASTING ALL YOUR ANXIETY ON HIM, BECAUSE HE CARES FOR YOU."
1 PETER 5:7

He cares for you—full time.

Week 21 Day 2: Gideons

He's falling behinder and behinder. This is the time of year lightbulbs usually come on. How can you flip his switch? You aren't the only one to notice his struggle, *he* also is realizing he's not keeping up with his buddies.

"'But Lord,' Gideon replied, 'how can I rescue Israel? My clan is the weakest in the whole tribe of Manasseh, and I am the least in my entire family.'" Judges 6:15 NLT

Your little Gideon is beginning to label himself the least of the least, and it breaks your heart. At the beginning of the year he came skipping and grinning into class, anticipating a good day. Now he drags himself in with eyes full of dread. Yes, he may never be a scholar but that doesn't mean he'll be a failure either.

"The Lord is with thee, thou mighty man of valor." Judges 6:12 KJV

How can you turn this around? How can you show him that he's a mighty man of valor, that he's so much more than the grade on a spelling test?

Find out what he's good at, what he likes, and give him opportunities to shine.

"Then the Lord turned to him and said, 'Go with the strength you have." Judges 6:14a NLT

What are his strengths? How can you differentiate for him? What about keeping him an hour after school once or twice a week to prepare him for the upcoming day? I know, neither of you want to do that, but you can make it positive. Give him snacks and let him talk. Use lots of encouraging words. Let him write on the board or use a special pen, use movement. Tell him secret information that will help him tomorrow. Make sure he knows you love him and believe in him.

Your little Gideon *is* a mighty man of valor. He will do great things. God has wonderful plans for his future, and you are a part of it.

Week 21 Day 3: Increasing

"AND JESUS KEPT INCREASING IN WISDOM AND STATURE, AND IN FAVOR WITH GOD AND MEN." LUKE 2:52

The Greek word translated as *increasing* means: to drive forward, to advance, grow, and profit. Like Jesus, our kiddos and we ourselves should be increasing—driving forward. You have goals for the year, and you are always driving forward to reach them. Let's take fractions for example. You teach what a fraction is, how to add and subtract them, how to reduce them, make common denominators, and so on. As you drive forward your kiddos increase. Occasionally you have to go back and reteach but even then, you are working toward increase. God is always working toward increase in us.

"SO THAT YOU WILL WALK IN A MANNER WORTHY OF THE LORD, TO PLEASE HIM IN ALL RESPECTS, BEARING FRUIT IN EVERY GOOD WORK AND INCREASING IN THE KNOWLEDGE OF GOD." COLOSSIANS 1:10

God wants us always increasing. Increasing in the knowledge of Him, love for Him, fear of Him, and surrender to Him; just to name a few. And like with fractions, we want our kiddos increasing in their relationship with God. We don't want asking Jesus into their hearts in kindergarten to be the end of their spiritual growth. We don't want the knowledge of Bible heroes to be as far as they get. Jesus, in His human nature, *kept* increasing and that's what we want for our kiddos. That's what God wants for us. How do we get there? By walking in a manner worthy of the Lord, by staying intimately connected through the day. How do our kiddos get there? All we can do is pray and model our genuine increasing relationship. What we *do* is so much more effective than what we say.

"THEIR CHILDREN WILL BE MIGHTY IN THE LAND." PSALM 112:2A NIV

Week 21 Day 4: Distant

You know God is in you. You know He's hovering over you, surrounding you, leading you, defending you, but goodness, He feels so distant. You press to get in His presence, and you feel Him, you do. But something just isn't right.

"THEREFORE REPENT, AND RETURN, SO THAT YOUR SINS MAY BE WIPED AWAY, IN ORDER THAT TIMES OF REFRESHING MAY COME FROM THE PRESENCE OF THE LORD." ACTS 3:19

You question yourself; are you harboring any unforgiveness, is there sin you haven't repented of? Probably not because you teach in a Christian School and you know how important those are. What you need is refreshing. How do you close the distance? Well, keep doing the right stuff. Stay in the Word, keep praying and praising.

"DRAW NEAR TO GOD AND HE WILL DRAW NEAR TO YOU." JAMES 4:8A

You're doing all the right things, but it doesn't seem to be working.

This is an exciting time of year academically but it's a difficult time of year mentally. Winter gloom has settled in and it looks like no let up for quite a while. You are working hard, finances are stretched, kids are sick, you're sick. There seems to be no light at the end of the tunnel and God feels distant. God *isn't* distant, you just need refreshing. Plan a fun day with your family or friends. Give yourself something to look forward to, something to get excited about. Feeling distant from God can be a symptom. Itchy eyes are a symptom of allergies. Feeling distant from God when you aren't distant is a symptom; you need refreshing. Refreshing takes time and you don't have time to spare, but you must make time or feeling distant will lead to depression. What would refresh you? I remember a couple times I drove to Walmart and sat in the car and had a good cry. That doesn't sound appealing, but oddly, it did refresh me. Get ice cream, go bowling, do something out of your rut.

"HE REFRESHES MY SOUL." PSALM 23:3A NIV

God wants to refresh you as badly as you want Him to. Win, win!

Week 21 Day 5: Permeate

If you teach 4th grade or up you probably keep some room spray on hand. There are times you need to permeate your room with a pleasant scent to counteract the other aromas permeating your room.

The other day when I was praying, I found myself using the word *permeate* a lot. "Lord permeate the hearts and minds of the kids. Permeate the atmosphere of our classroom, of our school. Please permeate the plans you have for us." Don't you love it when the Holy Spirit gives you a powerful word to pray?

"Do you not believe that I am in the Father, and the Father is in Me? The words that I say to you I do not speak on My own initiative, but the Father abiding in Me does His works." John 14:10

Jesus understands permeate. He is in the Father, the Father is in Him, and later in this passage He says we are in Him and He is in us. When you spray a scent in a room, the air is in the scent and the scent is in the air. They become one; the air is permeated but the scent dominates. I think that's what it's like when God permeates a situation. He completely saturates it with Himself, is completely *in* it, and dominates. So when I pray, "God please permeate the cancer in my friend's body," won't God completely diffuse Himself into the cancer cells? Won't He become one with them; be in them, and dominate? It reminds me of how He hovered over the waters in creation, brooding over them, moving upon them. But in this case, He isn't hovering over, He is hovering *in*. He becomes one with the problem and dominates!

"Yours, O Lord, is the greatness and the power and the glory and the victory and the majesty, indeed everything that is in the heavens and the earth; Yours is the dominion, O Lord, and You exalt Yourself as head over all." 1 Chronicles 29:11

He permeates.

Week 22

Week 22 Day 1: Arguments

"And after the earthquake a fire; but the Lord was not in the fire; and after the fire a still small voice." 1 Kings 19:12 KJV

Urgh. When will we learn to yield to that still small voice? We hear Him say, "Don't eat that." "Call Susie's mom." "Fill out those lesson plans." Simple words of grace. Words to save us trouble later down the road. And do we listen? Seldom. We argue. "Surely it won't hurt if I eat a little of this." "I'll deal with Susie's mom another day." "I'll do my lesson plans later." Then later, we break a tooth on the thing we ate, are confronted by an angry mom, and the administrator wanders in and looks over our plans—or lack thereof.

"Casting down arguments and every high thing that exalts itself against the knowledge of God, bringing every thought into captivity to the obedience of Christ." 2 Corinthians 10:5 NKJV

We argue and exalt *self*, letting our will run out the door like the kids at recess. Wisdom lives inside us; but so does selfishness and laziness. We shove Wisdom down and let selfishness float to the top when we're supposed to do the opposite. We tune our ear to what's in our head instead of our heart. Think of David and Bathsheba. He did not cast down his arguments and excuses and he got to the point he couldn't even hear the still small voice anymore. David, a man after God's own heart. And God had to send Nathan with the message He'd been saying all along. Arguing with the still small voice will drown Him out till He can't be heard at all.

Remember, Jesus was a teacher. He dislikes arguments as much as we do. He appreciates a good listener as much as you. Ok, so what do we do? We grab hold of today's new mercies and start fresh. We put on our *new creation* mantle and take off that dirty old garment of self we've been wearing. We ask for a clean heart and right spirit; determined that today we will listen and obey.

"For I determined to know nothing among you except Jesus Christ." 1 Corinthians 2:2a

Week 22 Day 2: Hitting the Rock

"As the people watch, speak to the rock over there, and it will pour out its water.... Then Moses raised his hand and struck the rock twice with the staff." Numbers 20:8b,11a NLT

Some years what you've done in the past just doesn't work with your current class. Moses caused himself a lot of heartache by trying to do things the way he'd done it before. God wanted to move in a different way.

As teachers, we must be willing to try new things. With one class you can model it once and they've got it. With another, you could model it a hundred times and they'd look at you with that blank look saying, "I don't get it." We can't keep hitting the rock because, unless God graciously intervenes like He did for Moses, the water won't come. This class needs manipulatives and T-charts and cooperative learning activities; differentiated instruction. You must focus on the "different" in differentiation. Do something different. Even though the lesson always worked before, this year you might have to let go. And it isn't always a low group that requires us to speak to the rock. Sometimes your group is so high they think acting out geometry terms is babyish. If you hit the rock, you'll lose them. This year you need to speak to the rock; geometry terms Headbands.

"And no one puts new wine into old wineskins. For the wine would burst the wineskins, spilling the wine and ruining the wineskins. New wine must be stored in new wineskins." Luke 5:37 NLT

Often in past years as a *mature* teacher I've asked the Lord to help me be a new wineskin. I don't want to get stiff and brittle and I know you don't either. Hitting the rock is easy. We've done it many times and it would be so much easier than trying something new. But we are not here for *easy*. We are here to make a difference and to serve the Lord. We are here to speak to the rock.

Week 22 Day 3: Yoked

"For My yoke is easy and My burden is light." Matthew 11:30

What are you yoked with? Guilt? Condemnation? A lack you see in yourself? The Lord has not given you a yoke of heavy burden. He has not given a yoke to weigh us down but to set us free. It sounds like an oxymoron but it's truth; the yoke Jesus offers is freedom. Imagine a big old solid oak yoke. The oak alone weighs nearly as much as a cross but then we are expected to pull in it. We are expected to pull our own weight. The burden of the weight alone is heavy but that's just the beginning, we must wear it all day while we work. This is the yoke the world gives us. Now imagine a yoke made of aluminum or light weight fiberglass. It sits on your shoulders like it was designed just for you. It's so light, you forget you're even wearing it, like eyeglasses. That is the yoke Jesus offers.

"Take My yoke upon you and learn from Me, for I am gentle and humble in heart, and you will find rest for your souls." Matthew 11:29

Like the kiddo in your class passing out his birthday treats. When he gets to his best buddy he points and says, "Take that one, it's the best." Jesus holds out a plate of desserts and says, "Take one." We get to choose our yoke, heavy or light. Jesus' yoke is gentle and restful. There is no tormenting condemnation with it. Accusation and fear are not part of Jesus' yoke.

The world tells you you're not doing enough, you're not good enough. Jesus says, "Let me pull the weight. Crawl into this yoke beside me and let me bear the burden." All He asks is that you walk beside Him.

Week 22 Day 4: Ape Arms

"Wherefore lift up the hands which hang down, and the feeble knees." Hebrews 12:12 KJV

You see her dragging her knuckles down the hallway as you lead your class to music. You aren't particularly close to her and you have plenty to do in your planning period, but you feel the Holy Spirit tug on your heart. She needs someone who will lift her hands which hang down, and she needs you because you understand her life, possibly better than her spouse.

I was reading Daniel chapter 10 yesterday. It's the story about the Prince of Persia delaying an angel from coming with the answer to Daniel's prayer. But this time I saw a different message. Daniel had been in mourning for three weeks. His arms hung down for twenty-one whole days. He was weak with the burden of it. Then an angel comes.

"'Don't be afraid,' he said, 'for you are very precious to God. Peace! Be encouraged! Be strong!' As he spoke these words to me, I suddenly felt stronger and said to him, 'Please speak to me my lord, for you have strengthened me.'" Daniel 10:19 NLT

The angel came, reached out, lifted Daniel, and spoke words of encouragement. The result? Daniel suddenly felt stronger. I was telling my kids what an awesome power we have when we use encouragement. The angel didn't zap Daniel with some supernatural spirit lifter, he merely reached out and touched him and said encouraging words. Encouragement is like a gift we can give or withhold. If we give it the result will instill hope, renew confidence, provide support.

So, you deliver your kiddos to music and hunt her down. You listen to her story, really listen because you know how it feels to be unheard. You hold her and you speak the angel's words, "You are precious to God." You pray with her and her strength returns. You do it because that's what you do. You are in this together.

Week 22 Day 5:
Oops

That little guy picking his nose, the girl with the ongoing craft project, they are all perfect in their parents' eyes. As a teacher you've learned, there are no perfect kids. Yes, they are all wonderfully and fearfully made. But they all sin. Often, the parents don't understand that. They honestly think their child is different from all others; smarter, more creative, and more holy.

Here's the problem. You become friends with the parents. You trust them to be on your team. But then you get caught up with false confidence in your friendship and "overshare." You cross the line. You tell them something unpleasant but true about their child. Oops. They just went from friend to worse enemy in less than thirty seconds. You have offended them, and you are in deep doo-doo.

"DEEPER AND DEEPER I SINK INTO THE MIRE; I CAN'T FIND A FOOTHOLD. I AM IN DEEP WATER, AND THE FLOODS OVERWHELM ME." PSALM 69:2 NLT

It's hard being professional all the time. We all slip now and then. Our motives are pure. We want the child to grow up to be their best, and we thought sharing this information would help. Some would say share it anyway and too bad if the parent is offended. The Lord told me years ago, "Keep the door open." Relationship is more important than making a point. Let God make the points. Let Him open the eyes of the parents. Let the child's own sin "find him out." Keeping a good relationship is important. You can't be light and salt if they are out in the parking lot criticizing you to other parents.

Another lesson I learned is, don't give advice unless it's asked for. When you give unsolicited advice, you are casting your pearls before the swine. They aren't ready for it. No matter how *friendly* you are with your parents, you must be professional.

Now you pray, humble yourself, and do your best to make amends. Apologize for offending them and tell them how much you love their kiddo because that's the truth.

"BUT SPEAKING THE TRUTH IN LOVE." EPHESIANS 4:15A

Truth, love, professionalism.

Week 23

 # Week 23 Day 1: Weary

Your class is especially hard this year. Teaching just isn't fun and you're bombarded with doubts, "Do I really want to keep doing this?" You feel like Captain Nemo, twenty thousand leagues under the sea in a tiny submarine, day after day. You throw out past fun activities. School is drudgery. You sigh, remembering years when teaching was a pleasure.

Wait a minute! You've thrown out all the fun stuff? Why? Because it's over their heads or they're too rowdy? Honey, you're shooting yourself in the foot.

"LET US NOT LOSE HEART IN DOING GOOD, FOR IN DUE TIME WE WILL REAP IF WE DO NOT GROW WEARY." GALATIANS 6:9

Logically, it seems like doing your favorite projects with this group will make you weary. But, in fact, removing all the things you enjoy about teaching is going to suck more life out of you than doing them.

"BUT THOSE WHO TRUST IN THE LORD WILL FIND NEW STRENGTH. THEY WILL SOAR HIGH ON WINGS LIKE EAGLES. THEY WILL RUN AND NOT GROW WEARY. THEY WILL WALK AND NOT FAINT." ISAIAH 40:31 NLT

Open your little bag of tricks and pull out the ones you enjoy. Cutting out all the fun will result in burn out. Maybe you can't do them all with this group, but you can do some. Maybe you can't soar, but you can probably walk! So you won't get your usual results with these kiddos, that's okay. Adjust your expectations—dare I say—lower them? The activities you love are the ones the kids will remember. Don't rob the shining stars in the class of pleasant memories because the majority are low or rowdy. Do it for the sweeties and do it for yourself. You need to feed the teacher inside you. Cutting out what you enjoy will starve you. Do the fun stuff even when it seems crazy, even when it's hard. You might not enjoy it as much as other years but with God's help, it will energize you. You will reap if you don't let yourself grow weary. It's a promise.

Week 23 Day 2: Can't Get No Satisfaction

At my school, special classes use the grades, E, S, and U, U indicating unsatisfactory. Sometimes we feel like giving ourselves a U. Not because we aren't doing a good job, but because we feel unsatisfactory inside, in our spirit. Our Report Card would read: Sense of Well-being—U.

We spend time with the Lord, keep up with the laundry at home, handle everything at school, and go to church. Why do we feel so unsatisfactory? We pray about it and ponder. It's not depression or discouragement. Days pass. *Why do I feel so unsettled?* What is it? And finally, when we are desperate, the answer comes. It is hunger. Ah, we vaguely remember praying for hunger. Now here it is, the gentle tugging in our heart to come up higher.

"BLESSED ARE THOSE WHO HUNGER AND THIRST FOR RIGHTEOUSNESS, FOR THEY SHALL BE SATISFIED." MATTHEW 5:6

What do we do about it? Read the Bible more? Spend more time in prayer? This is one of those "count it all joy" situations that seem a bit like an oxymoron. We asked for hunger and God gave it! He answered our prayer! Yippee! Now, please help, Lord, this doesn't feel good.

Wait. What did our verse say? We *shall* be satisfied? Oh good, God is doing this, and His first step is to nudge us out of satisfaction and into hunger. This dissatisfaction is a good thing.

"FOR I AM CONFIDENT OF THIS VERY THING, THAT HE WHO BEGAN A GOOD WORK IN YOU WILL PERFECT IT UNTIL THE DAY OF CHRIST JESUS." PHILIPPIANS 1:6

Spiritual hunger isn't about doing more works, it's about drawing nearer to God in our heart. Getting into His presence, focusing on Him, submitting, putting off self and clothing ourselves in Christ. Becoming more aware of Him and yielding to Him. It's about driving with Him and being on the playground with Him. Putting Him to the forefront of our thoughts instead of off to the side. Only that will satisfy.

Week 23 Day 3:
In the Hole

You overspent at Christmas, used bill money for other stuff, or the fridge bit the dust. Now you find yourself in the hole. Maybe you were expecting some money from somewhere and it didn't pan out and you don't know how you're going to get out of this mess. You blame yourself, you could have been more careful, you should have waited and saved. Perhaps you didn't do anything foolish, but suddenly you have unexpected expenses. You feel like there are holes in your pockets and money is running through them. We've all been there. But wait a minute. Aren't mercies new every morning? Isn't grace sufficient? Does doing something dumb nullify grace? No.

"'THEN I WILL REBUKE THE DEVOURER FOR YOU, SO THAT IT WILL NOT DESTROY THE FRUITS OF THE GROUND; NOR WILL YOUR VINE IN THE FIELD CAST ITS GRAPES,' SAYS THE LORD OF HOSTS." MALACHI 3:11

Remember, you have an enemy who comes to steal, kill, and destroy. Don't be ignorant of his devices. He wants to see you in the hole. He wants you to focus on money instead of God. He wants you to question God's faithfulness. When you find yourself in the hole, it's not time to curl up in the fetal position, it's time to fight. Stop thinking about how you got into this mess and think about the One who can get you out.

"THE LORD WILL MAKE YOU THE HEAD AND NOT THE TAIL, AND YOU ONLY WILL BE ABOVE, AND YOU WILL NOT BE UNDERNEATH, IF YOU LISTEN TO THE COMMANDMENTS OF THE LORD YOUR GOD." DEUTERONOMY 28:13A

Ask the Lord to rebuke the devourer for you. Don't stop tithing. You will be tempted, but don't do it. Ask the Lord before you spend anything. Walk in obedience. He wants to show you His wonderful love and faithfulness. He wants to give you testimonies.

"THE LORD GIVES GRACE AND GLORY; NO GOOD THING DOES HE WITHHOLD FROM THOSE WHO WALK UPRIGHTLY." PSALM 84:11B

The Lord delivers and provides; He is our ever-present help. As you turn to Him, He will get you out of the hole.

Week 23 Day 4: Before

"THE LORD HIMSELF GOES BEFORE YOU AND WILL BE WITH YOU; HE WILL NEVER LEAVE YOU NOR FORSAKE YOU. DO NOT BE AFRAID; DO NOT BE DISCOURAGED." DEUTERONOMY 31:8 NIV

What is coming up that you're dreading? A meeting with disgruntled parents? Your yearly observation? Whatever it is, the Lord goes before you. In difficult situations our loving God goes before you. Your scary unknown is not unknown to Him. Remember the Jeremiah 29 plans? The ones to give you hope and a future? God has gone before you and planned all the details. He has set you up for success not harm.

At one time my dad was a clockmaker. A clockmaker takes little gears and springs and fits them intricately together. He makes sure all the parts are secure and balanced. Then he gives the pendulum a nudge and off goes the clock, ticking away. God goes before you and fits all the gears and details together. All the skill you need—the help, the wisdom, and every spring and gear of grace, He will provide. It's all lined up waiting for you because He goes before us.

"AND MY GOD WILL SUPPLY ALL YOUR NEEDS ACCORDING TO HIS RICHES IN GLORY IN CHRIST JESUS." PHILIPPIANS 4:19

Our path is laid out and He has gone down ahead of us, making the way. He's prepared hearts and removed obstacles. Not only that, but He is *with* us. He whispers in our ear and gives us the right words. He gives us peace and clarity. There is a rest in that, if we will take it. Too often we feel it's irresponsible to rest in Him. Does a little fretting and worrying show our sincerity? No. Trust, obey, follow, pray, but don't worry.

"GOD IS OUR REFUGE AND STRENGTH, A VERY PRESENT HELP IN TROUBLE." PSALM 46:1

God goes before you. He knows what's coming and He's already prepared you. He's with you, holding your hand, speaking to your heart.

Go on, give that pendulum a nudge and get ticking.

Week 23 Day 5: Oh St. Valentine!

"But now faith, hope, love, abide these three; but the greatest of these is love." 1 Corinthians 13:13

Maybe I've taught too long but this holiday that's supposed to be about love—I don't like it. Sadly, it's more about candy, treats, and gifts than love. It's about getting more valentine cards than Benny. Love is about unselfish giving, but Valentine's Day is about getting. And the parents are no help; I ask one parent to bring in a sweet treat and I end up with ten dozen cookies and cupcakes! My daughter calls it the Christian Halloween. I think both Halloween and Valentine's Day should always be on Saturday. But that's not going to happen. So, what do you do about it?

"But the one who endures to the end, he will be saved." Matthew 24:13

You endure. You paste on a smile and go with the flow. Hopefully you actually like the holiday, but either way, you make the best of it. That's what you do because you love your kiddos. Even though you know there will be wildness and bragging and hurt feelings, you party on because you want them to have fun. You want them to have pleasant memories. You sneak "secret admirer" cards to kiddos you know won't get as many. (Even though you insist that everyone bring a card for every classmate.) You plant a secret surprise for the little one with disconnected parents. You obligingly raise the voice level, you plan energy draining games and brain breaks. You provide zip locks so they can take home all but two treats. As with Christmas, you do your best to focus their attention on Jesus, adding in His servant, St. Valentine.

You will go out of your way and way out of your comfort zone to make this a happy day because you love your kiddos. Love is what Valentine's Day is all about and loving your kids is what you're all about.

Week 24

Week 24 Day 1: Appearance

"Abstain from all appearance of evil." 1 Thessalonians 5:22 KJV

Why didn't the Lord just say, abstain from all evil? Evil is pretty straightforward, no gray area. But the *appearance* of evil is wishy-washy. It's like a shadow. A shadow doesn't have substance, neither does the appearance of evil. You might not be doing something evil but on the surface, without digging down, it appears evil.

Once, as a teen I was looking at new lipsticks. I pulled out my old lipstick to compare the colors. Then I capped it and put it back in my purse. It was a perfectly innocent thing. But the clerk thought I stole a lipstick and searched my purse. I had the appearance of evil.

Our behavior is to be so exemplary that there isn't even a shadow of evil. How do we teach this to our kids who are desperate to be cool? We model the Christian walk.

"So that you may become blameless and pure, children of God without fault in a warped and crooked generation. Then you will shine among them like stars in the sky." Philippians 2:15 NIV

We can't walk the fence or live in the gray zones. We are to shine like stars. We live to a higher standard, abstaining from even the *appearance* of evil. No compromise. I'm not talking legalism; legalism is self-righteousness. I'm talking about letting your light so shine before men that they may see (*appearance*) your good works (not evil) and glorify God. The kids have us under a microscope. We must make sure they only see genuine, authentic, humble Christianity.

"But evil men and impostors will grow worse and worse, deceiving and being deceived." 2 Timothy 3:13 NKJV

The headlights on my car have a film over them. When I turn them on they still shine, but through cloudiness. Let's let our light shine brightly; not through the cloud of worldly appearance but like a city set on a hill and let's teach it to our kids.

Can our kiddos impact the world if they compromise with it? Can we?

Week 24 Day 2: Resistance

In WWII The Resistance was an underground movement in countries occupied by Germany. Their purpose was to resist the enemy and help those being oppressed. The Resistance was the good guys fighting the bad guys. They were a hidden enemy to the Germans, doing their work behind the scenes. The Germans were a very evident enemy; the Resistance was an unseen enemy.

As you move forward through the school year you are bound to encounter some resistance. The source of your resistance is the devil. He brings confusion and turns people against you who you thought were on your side.

"For our struggle is not against flesh and blood, but against the rulers, against the powers, against the world forces of this darkness, against the spiritual forces of wickedness in the heavenly places."
Ephesians 6: 12

Maybe it's a parent, a coworker, or even a student. Suddenly someone you thought you had a good relationship with turns against you. Be alert and on guard. The people standing against you are not really the resistance, they are pawns being used by your enemy. Pray for them, do your best to stay in relationship with them. It is the enemy you must resist. Resisting the people he uses as roadblocks just adds to the confusion. You must use God's weapons. Don't listen to accusing, offended lies in your head and don't hate the people trying to block your path. Use Truth and Love, God's weapons.

We resist and conquer by staying in the Truth and in love. The truth is, we can do anything God calls us to do. The truth is, nothing and no one can separate us from God's love. The truth is, God has plans for us; plans the devil doesn't like. The truth is, God is able to perform what we commit to Him. And the truth is, God can turn the heart of a king and He can turn the hearts that oppose us.

"Submit therefore to God. Resist the devil and he will flee from you."
James 4:7

Be sure you're in the right resistance movement—God's resistance movement.

Week 24 Day 3: The Parking Lot Club

"But no one can tame the tongue; it is a ... deadly poison." James 3:8

More damage is done to a school in the parking lot than a bad teacher could ever do. One ticked off parent can have a heyday going from car to car airing their grievance. And social media is even worse, more far-reaching. How do we do damage control? Get your sneakers on.

"Every place on which the sole of your foot treads, I have given it to you, just as I spoke to Moses." Joshua 1:3

When the accuser of the brethren gets going, we must get walking. Time to walk the campus and pray. There's not much we can do in the physical realm to combat this kind of thing. We can try to be peace makers, but we can't control what people say in the parking lot or on social media. However, we can walk and take back the territory the enemy is trying to steal. Pray for healing of the offended hearts. Pray the Lord will stop the lying lips and hover over the campus and the situation, to establish His Kingdom and will. Ask that He work this together for good.

One year we arrived at school to find a big city TV truck in front of our small-town school. It was Grandparent's Day, a wonderful but stressful day, and now the TV station wanted to interview people because a disgruntled parent had called them. Talk about a bombshell. It was then we realized how crucial it is to defend our campus, to stay *prayed up*.

"If God is for us, who is against us?" Romans 8:31b

God is for us but Ephesians 6 tells us to stand our ground. We are to put on our full armor, pray, be alert, and persevere. We must not get lax in the defense of our school and our kiddos. Our enemy is a lion seeking someone to devour.

Be alert.

Week 24 Day 4: Cloak of Invisibility

You stand at the front of the classroom raising your voice and flapping your wings. No one sees you. Once again, somehow, you are covered in the cloak of invisibility. It's your worst fear. Worse than the dream about being naked in front of the class. This isn't a dream, it's reality.

"SHE SAID TO HERSELF, 'IF I ONLY TOUCH HIS CLOAK, I WILL BE HEALED.' JESUS TURNED AND SAW HER." MATTHEW 9:21–22a NIV

Jesus wasn't wearing a cloak of invisibility, His cloak carried healing. The woman seemed invisible. No one in the crowd seemed to notice her. Or maybe she just felt invisible—desperate to be seen and heard. You can relate. Just like the woman, you are not really invisible. Your voice is not silent. It's not you, it's your kiddos. Kids today have learned to tune things out. What do you do about it? You must eliminate all the other sounds that drown you out. Once you get the class down to zero noise, do what the woman did. Reach out to Jesus.

"HE WILL SEND HELP FROM HEAVEN TO RESCUE ME, DISGRACING THOSE WHO HOUND ME.... MY GOD WILL SEND FORTH HIS UNFAILING LOVE AND FAITHFULNESS." PSALM 57:3 NLT

Use the control and authority you have. Start taking away recess minutes; that nearly always buys you some quiet. When you get the class to silence, pray. God will send help from heaven. Did you hear that? Help from heaven! The hounding chaos will be routed out. God will send invisible help to rescue your invisible voice. He is unfailing and faithful. His cloak doesn't just heal, it helps in every way we need, even when help from heaven is required.

Week 24 Day 5: Double Portion Cloak

Up at 5, coffee, off to school, move Buddy's desk, assignments on the board, doc camera ready to go, bell work distributed, schedule checked for duties, look over Bible lesson and Math, think up anticipatory sets for both, run to teacher's devotions, then the restroom and it's 8:00. We're off. We are running like a fine-tuned clock, ticking away through our day. We're going through our daily routine, running on our own steam, leaning on our own understanding. Wait. What? Leaning on our own understanding? That's not good. We've lost the Divine edge. We've lost that something extra God provides for His teachers. Well, maybe lost is the wrong word. Packed away is more like it.

Do you have clothing in the back of your closet that you keep but never wear? Like a wedding gown? You have an affection for it, you value it, but it's packed away.

"Elisha picked up Elijah's cloak, which had fallen when he was taken up. Then Elisha returned to the bank of the Jordan River."
2 Kings 2:13 NLT

When God took Elijah to Heaven in a fiery chariot, He tossed Elijah's cloak down to Elisha. But before He did, He doubled the portion of Elijah's spirit on it for Elisha. God has a double portion cloak of anointing for you too. He drops it down, this cloak of unique anointing designed just for you. Somewhere along the way through this school year your cloak ended up in the back of your closet packed away; or worse yet, in the ever dreaded LOST AND FOUND!

You've been doing a good job with your own natural ability but with the Divine edge it could be so much better—more effective and fulfilling.

It's time to reach up once again and take hold of the cloak God designed just for you. The cloak that makes you more than ordinary, even more than exceptional. Unpack your cloak and cross that river on dry ground.

Week 25

Week 25 Day 1: A Place

It's the time of year you start thinking about next year. Will you stay at your school, at your grade level? Are you feeling like a change?

"IN MY FATHER'S HOUSE ARE MANY DWELLING PLACES; IF IT WERE NOT SO, I WOULD HAVE TOLD YOU; FOR I GO TO PREPARE A PLACE FOR YOU." JOHN 14:2

Whether you are feeling the winds of change or are happy to stay where you are, be assured, God always has a place for you. He goes before you and prepares a place, not just in Heaven, but here on earth too. Remember, He has plans for prosperity and hope. Remember how He hovered over the waters in creation, making plans and carrying them out?

Maybe it's a hard year and you're doubting your calling. Don't doubt it during a tough year. Difficulty does not mean you're not called. David went through lots of difficulty, but he was still anointed king. Moses had millions of difficult students, but he was still their deliverer. When God is moving you to a new place, He prepares your heart and He prepares the way. But in the meantime, in the limbo, while you listen for His direction, you feel sort of disconnected. Are you staying or going? Where is your place?

"THEY WENT AWAY AND FOUND A COLT TIED AT THE DOOR, OUTSIDE IN THE STREET; AND THEY UNTIED IT." MARK 11:4

The colt destined for Jesus' triumphal ride into Jerusalem on Psalm Sunday may have felt he didn't have a place. He was just tied up at a door. What kind of life is that? Little did he know; the disciples were on their way. Jesus had prepared a place for him. Jesus had wonderful plans for him. He probably felt stalled out, displaced, maybe even weary—like you. That was a temporary condition.

God already knows the plans He has for you. He has a place for you, and He will declare it to you. Just as He led Abraham from place to place, He will lead you to your place.

Let not your heart be troubled.

Week 25 Day 2: No Joy in Mudville

Unlike mighty Casey, you have not struck out. You have been hitting home runs left and right but somehow you are missing your joy. You walk into the classroom in the morning and realize there's a sort of invisible gloom. It tends to creep in somewhere around February; maybe because you are so done with winter and so ready for spring. But winter lingers on with its steely gray skies that mask the sun. You aren't depressed or discouraged. You just feel sort of blah in your spirit. It might be the spirit of heaviness.

"To console those who mourn in Zion, To give them beauty for ashes, The oil of joy for mourning, The garment of praise for the spirit of heaviness." Isaiah 61:3a NKJV

Praise is what banishes heaviness—a garment of praise. A garment is something you wear, not just singing a song of praise in the morning. This is wearing praise throughout your day. You are in a battle and praise is your weapon. Think of a person battling cancer; all day long they are fighting to overcome the disease. Their body is fighting, their mind is fighting, and their spirit is fighting. They wear their fight like a garment.

If you don't fight off the heaviness it will grow and continue even when spring arrives. Heaviness unchecked can lead to depression. It doesn't only affect you, it affects your kiddos. They become less tolerant of each other, there are more arguments on the playground. Your cooperative learning is less cooperative and more disruptive.

The spirit of heaviness comes in subtly, a little at a time. Unless you are alert you probably won't notice it for a while.

"Devote yourselves to prayer, keeping alert in it with an attitude of thanksgiving." Colossians 4:2

Alertness is an action of the mind and the mind is where the fight begins. Throughout the day keep your thoughts focused on praise. Look for God's character and grace. Crank up praise music and crank up a grateful heart. Cultivate praise in your kids. Make time to praise and thank God and time to praise and encourage each other. Change the atmosphere of the room from gloom to praise.

Week 25 Day 3: Eddie Haskell

Eddie was a character in the show *Leave It to Beaver* in the 1950's. He was the kid who was perfect and polite in front of adults but always sneaking and mischievous when no one was looking. Every now and then we have an Eddie Haskell in our classroom. You usually recognize them pretty early on. You know he's behind a lot of the rebellion in the classroom. He's respectful to your face but undermines your authority to the other kids.

"When people tried to bow before him, Absalom wouldn't let them. Instead, he took them by the hand and kissed them. Absalom did this with everyone who came to the king for judgment, and so he stole the hearts of all the people of Israel." 2 Samuel 15:5-6 NLT

The tricky thing here is that you can get pulled into a little silent war. Remember, the kids are not your enemy. Sometimes it can feel like it when you are worn down and weary. The kids are your flock of sheep, your mission field, but not your enemy, not even the Eddie Haskells. Yes, some of your sheep are naughty and manipulative. Don't sink to their level. You must stay above all that. Don't play their game. Remain professional.

The Lord God Almighty has dominion in your classroom. You are the authority He has placed over the kids. Declare this in your room each morning. Say the name of Jesus above every name. If your kids are old enough, do some Bible lessons on rebellion; what it is and how God feels about it. Pray for Eddie to have a clean heart and a right spirit and pray it for yourself. Get some other teachers to come to your room and pray. Change the atmosphere of the room. Ask the Holy Spirit to hover over your room birthing respect and the fear of God. Pray for your Eddie Haskells to have an encounter with God.

Stand your ground.

Week 25 Day 4: Guilt

You're up every day before the sun and work like a dog until well after it goes down. Do you feel good about that? No, you feel guilty that you're not doing enough, not working hard enough, not helping enough people, neglecting your family, friends, coworkers, and church. Ba-loney! It's ridiculous but that's how you feel.

"But there they are, overwhelmed with dread, where there was nothing to dread." Psalm 53:5a NIV

It's not enough that you work so hard, the enemy wants you to feel bad on top of it. He wants to rob you of the satisfaction of a job well done. After a day of pouring out all you have, the devil tells you it wasn't enough. I'm going to tell you something that is the opposite of what you say all day long. Do NOT Listen! Don't listen to the lies of the father of lies.

"And do not give the devil a foothold." Ephesians 4:27 NIV

Don't let yourself be weary in well doing. Weariness turns up the volume of the devil's voice, while making it harder to hear God's still small voice. And boy, are you weary. Teaching involves long hours, hard work, and the stress of supervising all the diverse little personalities in the class. You don't need to pile guilt on top of it. You should feel joy, not guilt.

"The master was full of praise. 'Well done, my good and faithful servant. You have been faithful in handling this small amount, so now I will give you many more responsibilities. Let's celebrate together!'" Matthew 25:21 NLT

The Lord sees that you are doing exceedingly abundantly more than anyone could imagine. He sees your long hours and the cries of your heart for your kiddos. In His eyes any lack on your part is as far as the east is from the west. He sees all the good; even the good no one else sees or appreciates. Everyday—every single day you bring Him glory. That's what He sees. And what He says is, "Well done."

Week 25 Day 5: More

"You have been faithful in handling this small amount, so now I will give you many more responsibilities. Let's celebrate together!"
Matthew 25:21b NLT

By this point in the school year you have entered the *more responsibilities* stage. It seems like the farther you get in the year, the fuller your plate gets. In fact, your plate is overflowing. It's probably time to clean off your plate a bit. Our plates are sort of magical. We start out with a well-organized plate: meat, peas, potatoes, fruit. Family, work, church, rest. Over the period of a few weeks it magically becomes a smorgasbord. In addition to your healthy balanced plate you have: Sauerkraut, olives, hashbrown casserole, and on and on. I don't know how it happens, but eventually you must call a halt to it.

"Stand your ground, and after you have done everything, ... stand."
Ephesians 6:13b NIV

God asks us to stand our ground. He has assigned us a certain portion of ground. It is just the right size for us to manage—or stand. I have a rather small yard because I don't enjoy yard work. My daughter and her husband love yard work. They have fruit trees, a garden, and a large grassy yard. God assigns each of us ground to stand that is the right size for us. If you are overwhelmed, you are most likely standing someone else's ground. If my daughter and I traded yards, both of us would be frustrated.

God gives us more responsibilities when we show Him we are trustworthy, but He does not give us more than we can stand. When the *many more responsibilities* become too many responsibilities it's time to remove some from our plate.

"I will open the windows of heaven for you. I will pour out a blessing so great you won't have room to take it in!" Malachi 3:10b NLT

God overwhelms us with blessings not responsibilities.

Week 26

Week 26 Day 1: Girded

"STAND FIRM THEREFORE, HAVING GIRDED YOUR LOINS WITH TRUTH."
EPHESIANS 6:14A

About ten more weeks in this school year. Are you keeping your loins girded? Girded was a way men tucked their robes into a belt to transform skirts into pants. They did this in order to fight more effectively.

This time of year, it's easy to get discouraged. You've fought the good fight, but it feels like you are losing ground.

"BUT SHAMMAH HELD HIS GROUND IN THE MIDDLE OF THE FIELD AND BEAT BACK THE PHILISTINES. SO THE LORD BROUGHT ABOUT A GREAT VICTORY."
2 SAMUEL 23:12 NLT

Are you girded and standing your ground or are you allowing weariness to rule? Shammah girded himself with truth like, *God is with me so I can stand.* The rest of David's army forgot their big girl panties and ran away. Truth girded Shammah. The God who split the Red Sea and drowned the Egyptian army was with him. The same God will bring victory for you.

Time is short. You're standing in a field of Lentils thinking, "How did I end up here in this crazy bean field?" Do you flee or stand? You've done everything but stand on your head to get these kiddos to learn their states and capitals. Will you give up or gird up? At one point the kids understood reducing fractions but now they're totally confused. Do you move on or gird up and start over again?

You gird up. That's what you do because you're a *good* teacher. David had lots of soldiers but Shammah wasn't any old soldier, he was extra good. The Bible labels him a mighty man. When others gave up, he stood and fought, and you will do the same because you aren't ordinary.

Take the evening off. Let the grading go or (gasp) throw it away. Tuck yourself up in the shadow of God's wing and let Him encourage you. He will give you ideas, inspiration, and courage. You need what He has more than another grade entered.

Gird your loins for heaven's sake.

Week 26 Day 2: Nightmares and Cares

You wake up in a cold sweat—another school dream. You are so passionately connected with your class that you don't even disconnect in your sleep!

"I SAW A DREAM AND IT MADE ME FEARFUL; AND THESE FANTASIES AS I LAY ON MY BED AND THE VISIONS IN MY MIND KEPT ALARMING ME." DANIEL 4:5

My daughter, also a teacher, had a dream I have to share. *She was in class and three men dressed completely in black, like ninjas, entered the room. She yelled to the children to get under their desks, jumped on the counter, and launched herself onto the men, knocking them to the ground. Just then the principal stepped in, "What are you doing, Miss B.? These are missionaries visiting from China."*

It's funny now, but she woke up in a panic. We've all been there. We love our kids and feel a weight of responsibility for them; even in our sleep we worry. We worry about doing the right or wrong thing. We worry about doing too little or too much. What is the solution to this problem? I don't know. It's the price we pay for passion.

"SO BECAUSE YOU ARE LUKEWARM, AND NEITHER HOT NOR COLD, I WILL SPIT YOU OUT OF MY MOUTH." REVELATION 3:16

We are not lukewarm—hot all the way. We can't disconnect from our kids or be lukewarm about them, even the stinkers. First, we don't want Jesus to spit us out of His mouth. And second, lukewarm is not our nature. Caring about the kids, about their cursive J, their safety in a lockdown, their dying kitty; it's all part of the gig. A friend recently said, "Teaching isn't a job, it's a life." Teaching is our life, identity, calling and purpose. It's the way we bring glory to the Lord. So, we shake off the nightmares, panic when we forget to send home their spelling list, keep fancy envelopes for teeth, and put band-aids on invisible owies. Why? Because no one will ever accuse us of being lukewarm.

We care, a little too much.

Week 26 Day 3: Letting Lame Men Walk

"SO THE CROWD MARVELED AS THEY SAW THE MUTE SPEAKING, THE CRIPPLED RESTORED, AND THE LAME WALKING, AND THE BLIND SEEING; AND THEY GLORIFIED THE GOD OF ISRAEL." MATTHEW 15:31

Sounds like your class: the crippled, lame, and blind. Of course, there's no mute. Mute is never a problem these days.

At church recently we sang a song with the words, "Letting Lame Men Walk." The word that struck me was *letting* and I've been thinking about it ever since. Letting, not making or healing. It sort of indicates something we could withhold. We can let/allow lame men to walk or not.

You have some lame men in your class: one who can't read, one who can't divide, one with dysgraphia, or turmoil at home. How can you *let* them walk? It will take more than differentiation. We need to differentiate but the results of differentiation are not instant; it will not get them up and walking right away.

"FOR A RIGHTEOUS MAN FALLS SEVEN TIMES, AND RISES AGAIN." PROVERBS 24:16A

If we don't quickly find a way to *let them walk*, they might give up, never rise again. We must find a way to encourage our lame ones. Think about what helps you on a hard day. A note of encouragement, a compliment from your boss, a surprise treat? The same things that let you walk on lame days will help them rise. Maybe you can't make them divide or read or write like the other kids, but you can allow them to walk. Your genuine compliments are jewels; look for opportunities to give them out. A teacher's note of encouragement can become a treasure. A piece of candy snuck into a grubby hand will lift a sad heart. Demonstrating your love, showing that you value them, that will let them walk.

"HE HAS SENT ME TO PROCLAIM FREEDOM FOR THE PRISONERS AND RECOVERY OF SIGHT FOR THE BLIND, TO SET THE OPPRESSED FREE." LUKE 4:18B NIV

Let the lame walk.

Week 26 Day 4: The Rehearsal

This rehearsal is not for the spring play or leading songs for chapel. This rehearsal is in your head. You are upset, offended, wounded, or angry. You lay in bed (not sleeping, of course) rehearsing what you should have said or what you could have said or what you might say. Call a hearse for the rehearsal!

"WE DEMOLISH ARGUMENTS AND EVERY PRETENSION THAT SETS ITSELF UP AGAINST THE KNOWLEDGE OF GOD, AND WE TAKE CAPTIVE EVERY THOUGHT TO MAKE IT OBEDIENT TO CHRIST." 2 CORINTHIANS 10:5 NIV

The hurts you rehearse are pretensions that set themselves against what God wants for you. Demolish them, don't rehearse them! God wants you to lay down in peace because He is with you. He is your vindication and Defender.

It's Satan who wants you up all night, stirring up your hurts, nursing bitterness and pity. This rehearsal is not a dress rehearsal; you have let your armor down and Satan is going after you with all his fiery darts. Come on, get into your armor. Put on your helmet, you have the mind of Christ and ears to hear the Holy Spirit. Slip into your breastplate, be forgiving, set your heart to righteousness. Lift your shield, quench those fiery darts, move mountains. Draw your sword of the Spirit, "Create in me a clean heart, O God; and renew a right spirit within me." Buckle on your good news shoes. Along with the good news about Jesus is the good news that He will never leave you and nothing can separate you from His love!

Stop the rehearsal and start forgiving. You know you will eventually forgive, you might as well start now and get a good night's sleep. It's not your nature to hold a grudge, you're a teacher, you're above that. Even when your hurt is justified you let it go because you are a professional. You are called and anointed, and this problem? It's God's problem.

"THE LORD WILL FIGHT FOR YOU WHILE YOU KEEP SILENT." EXODUS 14:14

Let it go. You will because you must. You're a teacher.

Week 26 Day 5: The Performance

Yesterday we talked about rehearsing lines we would like to say to people who hurt us and how God is our vindication and Defender. I want to continue that theme because it is not easy to release our hurts, especially justified hurts.

"ONLY BY YOUR POWER CAN WE PUSH BACK OUR ENEMIES; ONLY IN YOUR NAME CAN WE TRAMPLE OUR FOES. I DO NOT TRUST IN MY BOW; I DO NOT COUNT ON MY SWORD TO SAVE ME. YOU ARE THE ONE WHO GIVES US VICTORY OVER OUR ENEMIES." PSALM 44:5-7A NLT

Our verse is about trampling enemies. Sadly, it's probably not an enemy who has hurt you. The deepest hurts come from those we care about. Do we want to trample the one who offended us? No. I chose this verse because it illustrates the best course of action. It's not our bow or sword—our words—that will bring victory, it's God's power and Name.

Once my second grade class had a basketball game with another Christian School second grade. One of my kiddos would get the ball, run down the court, pass the ball and zip ahead, catch his own pass, and try to make a basket. He didn't really need any other players; he was a team all by himself! The only problem was, he couldn't score. He could do it all, except score—the most important thing.

When we rehearse our woulda-shouldas, we are using our own bow and shield. We are little Joey, a team all our own. The trouble is, we will never score. All we do is waste time and emotion. We need to pass the ball to someone who can score. Pass the hurt to the Lord. It is His power and His Name that will push back the offense. It's only by His power we can forgive and move on. It's His Name above the name of hurt, injustice or frustration that overcomes. Any words we say, or excuse we make is like passing the ball to our self.

He is "the one who gives us victory."

Week 27

Week 27 Day 1: Your Dominions

Every year since 1980 I have read *The Lion, the Witch, and the Wardrobe* so my idea of dominion was skewed. In the story the witch rules over her dominions, Narnia, and calls herself the queen, so I assumed dominions were the same as kingdoms. I was wrong.

"FOR HE HAS RESCUED US FROM THE DOMINION OF DARKNESS AND BROUGHT US INTO THE KINGDOM OF THE SON HE LOVES." COLOSSIANS 1:13 NIV

A Kingdom has a supreme ruler. A Dominion is merely an influence. Kingdom is supreme—far above influence.

Have you had a student who needed rescue from the dominion of darkness? You wouldn't think we'd deal with that in a Christian School, but we do. They are a constant disruption; they battle you for control of the class. You know it's not flesh and blood behavior but a dominion of darkness. I had a student once who lived in an area well known for witchcraft. She brought darkness in with her every day. Every day I would kick it out, welcome the Holy Spirit, pray over her desk, and anoint it with oil. I was desperate. I thought I was dealing with something super powerful. It *was* powerful but not in comparison to God's power.

I have a leaky shower head at home. It leaks about a drop an hour. It has an influence but very limited, like a dominion. Niagara Falls is supreme: 681,750 gallons of water flow over one section of Niagara Falls per second. God's kingdom cannot be compared to a dominion. God's kingdom is exceedingly abundantly above a dominion.

So, what do you do about that student? You keep loving and fighting. But don't fight in fear and trepidation; fight like you're fighting in a kingdom more powerful than Niagara Falls. Love and fight for that child with bold confidence, not doubt. It is God's power that will rescue the child, not yours. Your job is to turn the faucet of Niagara Falls on. It's God's will that none should perish. He is our Deliverer. He will do it.

"THE ONE WHO CALLS YOU IS FAITHFUL, AND HE WILL DO IT."
1 THESSALONIANS 5:24 NIV

Week 27 Day 2: Coal

Do you have that little kiddo who seems like a lump of coal? Just going through the motions, not really interested or impressed by anything you do? He doesn't raise his hand, she participates only enough to not cause waves, he never excels, she endures the day. You wonder what will ever become of them?

There are two things about a lump of coal, it is formed by pressure and it's just a rock until fire is applied. It's our job to employ the right amount of pressure and to light a fire under our coal lump.

Being a former lump of coal, I know a little about motivating them. One year I moved mid-year from Chicago to rural Iowa. At school in Chicago the radio taught us French and read us *The Wheel on the School!* It was all very high tech. We learned a new style of cursive and did amazing art projects. In Iowa they were multiplying and dividing and doing old fashioned cursive. No French, no art, no *Wheel on the School*. All I enjoyed about school was gone and I was overwhelmed with the math. I became a lump of coal.

"THE LORD THEIR GOD WILL SAVE HIS PEOPLE ON THAT DAY AS A SHEPHERD SAVES HIS FLOCK. THEY WILL SPARKLE IN HIS LAND LIKE JEWELS IN A CROWN." ZECHARIAH 9:16 NIV

We've talked about this before, but we must find out what makes our lump of coal sparkle. Every jewel in a crown sparkles Motivating their sparkle is our job.

"I WILL GIVE YOU THE TREASURES OF DARKNESS AND HIDDEN RICHES OF SECRET PLACES, THAT YOU MAY KNOW THAT I, THE LORD, WHO CALL YOU BY YOUR NAME, AM THE GOD OF ISRAEL." ISAIAH 45:3 NIV

God has given us these treasures with hidden riches. He knows them by name and made them. Ask Him to open your eyes to see what makes them sparkle. Ask Mom and Dad; or Grandma—all she sees is sparkle! Don't let a week pass without giving everyone a chance to sparkle. Someday you'll be very glad you did.

Week 27 Day 3: Avails Much

You have prayed and prayed over this child with very little result. You wonder if your prayers are heard or if you're praying the wrong words or lacking fervency, or maybe you aren't righteous enough.

"THE EFFECTIVE, FERVENT PRAYER OF A RIGHTEOUS MAN AVAILS MUCH." JAMES 5:16B NKJV

Prayer is not a recipe that will flop if you don't get it quite right. God will not reject prayers because you didn't whip up enough fervor. This verse is referring to earnest sincere prayer; you know, the kind you pray for your kiddos all the time. When my son was little he prayed, "Thank you for mom and dad and our house and the cats and grass and the cracks in the sidewalk…." His prayers were fervent, fervently hoping to stay up later, but not earnest. It's the prayers from your heart that will avail much. So why aren't you seeing this child's situation improve?

Our prayer is like reaching out and turning a doorknob that opens the door for God to come on the scene. Every time we pray, we open the door. Whatever we say, whether eloquent or stumbling, it turns the knob to let God in.

"AFTER THESE THINGS I LOOKED, AND BEHOLD, A DOOR STANDING OPEN IN HEAVEN." REVELATION 4:1A

Our prayers open the door to heaven but that doesn't mean we see the answer immediately. Many times God answered my prayers for a child after I sent them on to their new teacher. We are dealing in things unseen. By faith we believe that we are availing much. One year I had a kiddo whose parent was bad off, on drugs. I prayed and prayed, fervently, earnestly, upside down, every way I knew how. Didn't see anything. Two years later that parent got saved! My prayers had availed much but I couldn't see it till the right time.

Your prayers are heard, and they are working. The door is already standing open.

"AND LET US NOT GROW WEARY WHILE DOING GOOD, FOR IN DUE SEASON WE SHALL REAP IF WE DO NOT LOSE HEART." GALATIANS 6:9 NIV

Week 27 Day 4: The Right Rx

"Each year Elkanah would travel to Shiloh to worship and sacrifice to the Lord of Heaven's Armies." 1 Samuel 1:3a NLT

"Are you tired, run-down, listless? Do you poop out at parties? Are you unpopular? The answer to all your problems is in this little bottle. Yes. Vitameatavegamin." The old I Love Lucy skit may very well describe how you're feeling. But instead of yucky tasting medicine, the prescription for our trouble is "The Lord of Heaven's Armies!" Tired, run-down, listless? The Lord of Heaven's Armies is the lifter of our face and the arms that hang down. Poop out at parties? The Lord of Heaven's Armies renews our strength and fills us with a river of life. Unpopular? The Lord of Heaven's Armies grants us favor with God and man. The solution to every problem? The Lord of Heaven's Armies.

"He saved us, not on the basis of deeds which we have done in righteousness, but according to His mercy, by the washing of regeneration and renewing by the Holy Spirit." Titus 3:5

Regeneration and renewing. The Lord is a fountain of youth; a fountain not hidden or run dry. A fountain always available to us. This time of year it's a great comfort to know we have an army on our side. And with that army, an Almighty General. We might feel weary of battle because, honey, as teachers we are always in a battle. But our General provides all we need: strength, wisdom, help, regeneration. In Him there is no lack. He alone is more than enough. He alone is exceedingly abundantly more than enough. And along with exceedingly abundantly more, He provides an army—a vast army—of angels to fight on our behalf.

"And the Lord opened the servant's eyes and he saw; and behold, the mountain was full of horses and chariots of fire all around Elisha." 2 Kings 6:17b

We may feel weary and alone, but we are not, oh, we are not. The Lord of Heaven's Armies is our Father.

Week 27 Day 5: Standing Firm

"AND THE PRIESTS WHO CARRIED THE ARK OF THE COVENANT OF THE LORD STOOD FIRM ON DRY GROUND IN THE MIDDLE OF THE JORDAN WHILE ALL ISRAEL CROSSED ON DRY GROUND, UNTIL ALL THE NATION HAD FINISHED CROSSING THE JORDAN." JOSHUA 3:17

You are nearing the promised land of summer vacation. Nearing, but not there. You still have this Jordan River of the last quarter to cross. In some ways it's the hardest quarter because somebody let the cat out of the bag to the kids and they also know summer is near. So, like the brave priests of Joshua's day, you pick up the ark and step out into the flooded river. Even though you are near the promised land, it's not going to be easy. You have to stand in the river holding the heavy ark of subject matter yet to teach while millions pass by. You are the reason everyone isn't swept away into chaos. So, you patiently stand, facilitating everyone's safe crossing to the next grade.

Joshua's priests had to stand while all the people and livestock crossed, and then wait while they collected big stones for monuments, and then stand some more while they *built* the monuments. There's a lot of standing left in this year: preparing for testing, big projects, field day, field trips, Mother's Day gifts, and meeting your spiritual goals for your kiddos. You've got a lot to accomplish while holding it all together. The weight of it gets heavier the longer you stand but you stand firm because you know monuments are being built.

"THEN JOSHUA SET UP TWELVE STONES IN THE MIDDLE OF THE JORDAN AT THE PLACE WHERE THE FEET OF THE PRIESTS WHO CARRIED THE ARK OF THE COVENANT WERE STANDING." JOSHUA 4:9

Where your feet stand, monuments are being built. In the future, children will remember the stones, the foundations you built, the helping verb song, the bug collection, the map project, the Bible story that touched their heart. Stones you lay without even realizing they're monuments. Precious stones you lay because that's what you do. And they will remember, yes, they will remember.

"NOW IF ANY MAN BUILD ON THE FOUNDATION WITH GOLD, SILVER, PRECIOUS STONES...." 1 CORINTHIANS 3:12

Week 28

Week 28 Day 1: Panic!

Last night you laid awake in horror at the volume of material you need to cover this last quarter.

"So do not worry about tomorrow; for tomorrow will care for itself. Each day has enough trouble of its own." Matthew 6:34

In thirty-six years of teaching I only finished my entire curriculum one year. It was the year I had the perfect class.

As educators our goal is quality, not quantity. What do your kiddos need to get from your class? Start with your spiritual goals. What passion do you hope to pass on to them? A love of God's Word? A heart for Missions? Make that your Bible-time focus. In academics, what do they need to succeed next year? Make sure you cover that. Don't stress over the rest.

When God led Moses and the children of Israel around the desert forty years, His focus was on learning, not getting to the end. He was all about refining, not speed. If you end the year with lessons untaught and pages undone, that's okay. Just do the best you can. If your kiddos leave fourth grade knowing long division and fractions, you've done well. Next year's teachers will review before they launch out into new stuff. These next six weeks focus on what's most important. Then the last few weeks have fun with stuff that's not so crucial. Remember the kiddos quit about three or four weeks before school ends.

Now is not the time to panic. Now is the time to create a few more wonderful memories with this bunch of youngsters. Enjoy these last days, this last quarter. If it's been a tough year, relax a little, take some pressure off yourself. You have one more fresh start; nine more weeks to love and pour into this group. All year you have been working hard, building this amazing hot fudge sundae and now it's time to put the cherry on top.

"Therefore, my beloved brethren, be steadfast, immovable, always abounding in the work of the Lord, knowing that your labor is not in vain in the Lord." 1 Corinthians 15:58 NKJV

Week 28 Day 2: Bloom's Taxonomy

"YOU CALL ME TEACHER AND LORD; AND YOU ARE RIGHT, FOR SO I AM." JOHN 13:13

I've been reading through the gospels lately and noticing what a good teacher Jesus was. He was pretty limited without smart technology and doc cams or even slates. He did draw in the sand once. He used what He had as effectively as possible. It seems to me He was aiming for the second level of Bloom's Taxonomy: understanding. As I read, second-level Bloom's words kept coming to mind: describe, explain, paraphrase, restate, summarize, show, demonstrate. Normally these are words we use to have the kids reveal their learning achievement. Jesus taught toward understanding by describing, explaining, restating (parables), etc. In John 3 Jesus uses childbirth, something Nicodemus was familiar with, to help him *understand* spiritual rebirth.

I've heard people say, "The teacher is the curriculum." Now, I'm fully in favor of having a good curriculum because if I'm the curriculum, we are seriously limited. Good curriculum is written by people much more knowledgeable than me. But I get what they mean. A teacher is the curriculum in that they communicate or transmit the knowledge to the student. You can have a poor curriculum, but a good teacher can make it effective. Jesus was definitely the curriculum!

"THE EARTH IS THE LORD'S AND THE FULNESS THEREOF; THE WORLD, AND THEY THAT DWELL THEREIN." PSALM 24:1 KJV

Jesus knows everything, from how to make a universe to how to make a mustard seed. He knows everything seen and unseen. But what amazes me is, with His vast knowledge beyond what we could even think or imagine, He is able to teach us. He is able to help us *understand*.

"THE SPIRIT OF THE LORD IS ON ME, BECAUSE HE HAS ANOINTED ME TO PROCLAIM GOOD NEWS TO THE POOR." LUKE 4:18a NIV

Jesus took an old testament scroll and explained to the people of His day how He fulfilled the prophecy. He related it to their lives so they could understand. He used methods we still use today. Jesus was the curriculum and you are the curriculum, the bridge to your student's understanding.

Week 28 Day 3: Fire Drill

It comes every month and yet it's always a surprise. The alarm blasts the air and for a second the world stops. All eyes turn toward you. In that split second your kiddos read calm confidence in your face and like a well-oiled machine, they move out the door. Month after month, year after year, you train the kids how to respond to the alarm. You practice exiting in various scenarios, from the gym, from the chapel, the restroom. When the alarm sounds, they look to you and they move.

"I WILL LIFT MY EYES TO THE MOUNTAINS; FROM WHERE SHALL MY HELP COME?" PSALM 121:1

Just as the kids look to you in a drill or lock-down situation, so should we look to our Help. Our first response to a problem should be to look to the Lord, and not panic. Like a fire drill, we need to practice. Paul exhorts us to pray without ceasing. Pray when you drive and when you walk, pray in the morning and at bedtime. Stop and pray for the class when they are confused or upset. Use any excuse to pray. Let the kids see you respond to need with prayer just as you respond to a fire alarm by moving. Let them see you look to the mountains where your Help comes from.

"WITH ALL PRAYER AND PETITION PRAY AT ALL TIMES IN THE SPIRIT, AND WITH THIS IN VIEW, BE ON THE ALERT WITH ALL PERSEVERANCE AND PETITION FOR ALL THE SAINTS." EPHESIANS 6:18

Look up!

Week 28 Day 4: Triage

We live so much of our lives with a triage mentality, dealing first with the most urgent needs. I was talking to a triage teacher friend the other day. Her pastor asked her what she was doing for self-care. She said, "Well, I get my nails done sometimes." Isn't that the way? We are so busy with triage we don't consider our own needs. There's family, school, church, the list goes on and on—and we are not even on our own list! I'm all for getting my nails done now and then, but that is not self-care! The question is, do we know what self-care is? I didn't, so I Googled it. Here are some self-care suggestions: 1. Exercise and eat healthy. More things to feel guilty about. 2. Reduce stress. Are you laughing? Reduce stress! What a joke.

In the triage of our lives there is no room for self-care and trying to squeeze it into our stress-filled lives adds more stress!

"CREATE IN ME A CLEAN HEART, O GOD, AND RENEW A RIGHT SPIRIT WITHIN ME." PSALM 51:10 KJV

We need a fresh attitude towards our triage. Step one, cross everything possible off your "to do" list. Our lives are full; pretty much everything we do is essential. The first step toward self-care is a right spirit toward our responsibilities. How can we make our day fun? How can we squeeze pleasure into the things we *have* to do? Psalm 51:10, *Clean up my heart, my grumpy, strength-sapping heart, and make my attitude right.*

By this time in the school year you may have lost the pleasure in teaching to the battlefield of daily life. It's time for self-care. Do something you've been wanting to do, a special themed day. The kids will like it, but you will too. It becomes self-care. Take a minute and figure out how to make that Math or Language lesson more fun. The kids will benefit, and so will you!

Bring on the clowns!

Week 28 Day 5: Priority Prayers

How do you pray for your kiddos? I go through the room most mornings and quickly pray over each child's desk. But I struggle in trying to pray specific Spirit led prayers for each kiddo. I worry my prayers are shallow. I want to pray meat, not milk and depending on the size of your class, this can be very time consuming.

"THE TWENTY-FOUR ELDERS FELL DOWN BEFORE THE LAMB, EACH ONE HOLDING A HARP AND GOLDEN BOWLS FULL OF INCENSE, WHICH ARE THE PRAYERS OF THE SAINTS." REVELATION 5:8B

I want my prayers to be worthy of a golden bowl. When the Lord tips those bowls years down the road, I want good stuff to come out.

When my daughter was pregnant, she was on bed rest for several months. The wonderful ladies of our church brought meals every evening. All the meals were good, but some were outstanding; some ladies brought pie for dessert.

I want the prayers for my students to be pie. So, after years of feeling guilty that I wasn't doing right by my kids, I decided to go for pie—quality, not quantity. I start at student number one and work forward doing several each day and when I get to the end of the list, I start over again. Some days I do seven, some days one, but every day I feel satisfied that I have touched God's heart for my kids. Do I ever go out of order? Of course. We are running a triage here. Urgent needs come up. But for the most part I offer up a pretty steady diet of pie.

"FOR THIS REASON, SINCE THE DAY WE HEARD ABOUT YOU, WE HAVE NOT STOPPED PRAYING FOR YOU. WE CONTINUALLY ASK GOD TO FILL YOU WITH THE KNOWLEDGE OF HIS WILL THROUGH ALL THE WISDOM AND UNDERSTANDING THAT THE SPIRIT GIVES, SO THAT YOU MAY LIVE A LIFE WORTHY OF THE LORD AND PLEASE HIM IN EVERY WAY: BEARING FRUIT IN EVERY GOOD WORK, GROWING IN THE KNOWLEDGE OF GOD." COLOSSIANS 1:9–10 NIV

Week 29

Week 29 Day 1: Aroma

"Collect choice spices—12 1/2 pounds of pure myrrh, 6 1/4 pounds of fragrant cinnamon, 6 1/4 pounds of fragrant calamus, and 12 1/2 pounds of cassia." Exodus 30:23–24a NLT

You walk in on Monday morning and a sweet smell meets you. You're home. Well, you're at school but that welcoming smell feels like home. Every school has it. Churches don't have it, malls don't, doctor's offices don't. No other place where people gather smells quite like a school. I've tried to figure out exactly what it is. I think it's a mix of Ticonderoga pencils, left over lunches, feet, the lack of deodorant, and twelve and a half pounds of the scent pods you use to try to cover up the other smells. I suspect there is even the lingering scent of mimeo from decades past. Ahhh. When it all comes together it's a wonderful thing.

When we moved from Illinois to Arizona we thought the rain produced a terrible stink. Instead of smelling like cornfields and fertile soil, the rain smelled of creosote, mesquite, and other desert plants. We held our breath and wrinkled our noses. After a few months though, we'd rush out into the rain, take a deep breath, and savor the wonderful clean fragrance. Somehow the stink had turned to perfume. I don't really understand it. Maybe it's because rain is so precious to us. But it's the same phenomenon with school smell. My friend's husband would walk in and say, "Whew, how do you stand this smell? It stinks!" We walk in after a break or at the end of summer and think it's a wonderful aroma.

Why? How does the magic work? It might be the same as Arizona rain, it's precious. School smell reminds us of something precious: lives changing, growth, learning, sweet faces. And maybe there's more. Maybe mixed in with the smells of moldy oranges, band aids, and crayola is our own blood, sweat, and tears. Take a deep breath. Smell it? It's you, pouring out your love, anointing, and your very being in this place.

"For we are a fragrance of Christ to God." 2 Corinthians 2:15a

Week 29 Day 2: Peace, Pursue it!

"They must turn from evil and do good; they must seek peace and pursue it." 1 Peter 3:11 NIV

This time of year everyone begins to get a little tired of each other. The kids bicker like siblings and frankly, we feel a little annoyed by a coworker or two. In a small school we know each other so well, and after nearly nine months together we get weary of idiosyncrasies. We are all tired, not just of each other, but tired from tiptoeing around the little personalities in our classes, tired of state standards and objectives, tired of stacks of grading, tired of questioning parents, tired of school. We must not make our fellow soldiers scapegoats for our frayed nerves.

"Make every effort to keep the unity of the Spirit through the bond of peace." Ephesians 4:3 NIV

When the iron sharpening iron begins to start a fire, it's time to do something about it. When the critical thoughts and annoyances come to our mind, we must resist. The Accuser of the brethren wants to use our weary condition to stir up strife.

"But avoid foolish controversies and genealogies and strife and disputes about the Law, for they are unprofitable and worthless." Titus 3:9

Strife is unprofitable and worthless; and even worse, it is destructive and dangerous. Strife gives Satan a foothold. When the thoughts and irritations come, we must turn them into profit instead of loss. Do the opposite of what Satan wants, pray for those who annoy us.

"But I tell you, love your enemies and pray for those who persecute you." Matthew 5:44 NIV

Ok, the coworkers who annoy you are not necessarily persecuting you, they are more like thorns in the side, but still the solution is to fight back. Fight back in prayer. Prayer will restore unity because unity is God's will for your school. Maybe the annoyance will lessen or maybe your attitude will change. Either way, prayers bring peace!

Week 29 Day 3: Leper

"He lifted me out of the slimy pit, out of the mud and mire; he set my feet on a rock and gave me a firm place to stand."
Psalm 40:2 NIV

You managed to tick off the wrong mom. You didn't do anything wrong, but she chose to be offended and now you are the subject of discussion for the parking lot club. You are a leper; the other moms look at you differently. Unclean, unclean! You have bent over backwards to help this child but somehow Mom thinks you are unfair, and she has thrown you in a pit. And, good grief, some of the teachers are even looking at you funny!

"When they cry out to the Lord because of their oppressors, he will send them a savior and defender, and he will rescue them."
Isaiah 19:20b NIV

Stay calm, you have a Defender. If you reach up to Him, He will lift you out of this pit. It is no fun being the target of gossip.

Generally, these things pass over in time. It's important though to reach up to the Lord so the Accuser of the brethren doesn't run rampant. Get some prayer backup and put on your full armor of God. If you are not totally innocent in the situation, make it right. Do what you need to do to derail the gossip train. The Lord will be with you and He will set you on firm ground again. Be genuine and authentic. Don't let pride into the mix. The Hebrew word for *pit* in this verse means a pit of destruction. Don't let this thing get out of hand. Reach up to the Lord, let your administrator know what's going on, do what you need to do ethically to restore peace, stay professional, and don't let yourself become offended. It's the Lord's place to defend and rescue you.

"The one who calls you is faithful, and he will do it."
1 Thessalonians 5:24 NIV

Week 29 Day 4: Sealed

"AND DO NOT GRIEVE THE HOLY SPIRIT OF GOD, WITH WHOM YOU WERE SEALED FOR THE DAY OF REDEMPTION." EPHESIANS 4:30 NIV

This is one of my favorite promises for my prodigal students. They are sealed with the Holy Spirit. They asked Jesus into their hearts at a young age and they were sincere. They received the Holy Spirit at that time, and they were sealed.

Have you read *Frindle* by Andrew Clements? When the main character is in fifth grade his teacher writes him a letter, seals it, doesn't let him read it, but has him sign and date the envelope. Many years later he receives the sealed letter and it reveals truth about his fifth-grade experience. The letter had not been tampered with, the seal was not broken, what was originally put in the envelope was preserved. Over many years and life experiences the original message remained the same because it was sealed.

Your kiddos receive Christ. God has plans for them. His plans, his message, his gifts are sealed in them with the Holy Spirit. That kiddo who starts smoking pot in middle school, who gets in with the wrong crowd, who becomes a parent too young? Those kiddos are sealed. Their mistakes and bad choices don't unseal God's message—His Spirit.

Many of us had seasons where we stepped away from God or drifted down stream a way. But here we are, serving the Lord in full-time ministry, teaching. We were sealed. We might not have been aware of it, but we were sealed just the same.

"FOR GOD'S GIFTS AND HIS CALL ARE IRREVOCABLE." ROMANS 11:29 NIV

You and your kids are sealed. Nothing can separate either of you from the unfailing, faithful, love of God.

Week 29 Day 5: Heard

We often feel unheard. We repeat directions twenty times and still a kiddo says, "What are we supposed to do?" We ask everyone to stand for the pledges and no one stands. We tell the parents to send lunches for the field trip and two kids arrive with no lunch. We report the restroom is out of paper towels. Six hours later, still no paper towels. Our voice is invisible, unheard. Or so it seems.

"JESUS ANSWERED, 'I AM THE WAY AND THE TRUTH AND THE LIFE.'" JOHN 14:6 NIV

Jesus answered. If He answered, it means He heard. He responded immediately. Cause and effect; we cry out, He answers. Kids, parents, administration, our own families don't hear us, but Jesus does. In fact, He hears the cry of our heart before we put it to words. Psalm 139:1 tells us God knows our thoughts even when we are far away. He hears us. He understands our frustration.

"THOMAS SAID TO HIM, 'LORD, WE DON'T KNOW WHERE YOU ARE GOING, SO HOW CAN WE KNOW THE WAY?'" JOHN 14:5 NIV

How many times have we felt like Thomas, "Where are you, Lord, and where are you going?" God responds to us just as He did to Thomas, "Jesus answered." The Lord hears and answers when no one else does. He is the Way, the Truth, and the Life, and He hears us. He is the Way when our classroom management disappears and chaos erupts. He is the Truth when we are confused and when we doubt our calling. He is the Life on a windy Friday afternoon when we feel defeated.

One cold February evening when one of my daughters was a baby, she got very sick. After much prayer we ended up in the hospital. I stood beside her steel crib on frozen feet feeling unheard but calling out, "Lord do you even hear my prayers? Do you even care?" Late that night a coworker came by. She entered the room apologetically, a little uncomfortable. "The Lord told me to bring you these." She reached in her purse and pulled out a pair of warm wooly socks! The Lord did care, He knew my feet were blocks of ice and He sent someone out on a cold winter night to bring me a pair of socks!

Your voice is not invisible to God. He hears and He answers.

Week 30

Week 30 Day 1: Ok

How many times have you written *Good* or *Ok* at the top of a paper because it wasn't great? I'm afraid, in a teacher's mind *Good* has become not so good.

"For the Lord is good; His lovingkindness is everlasting And His faithfulness to all generations." Psalm 100:5

Often we say, "God is good," and the response is, "All the time." We say it without thinking. We need a selah moment here. "God is good," is not a cliché to throw around lightly. "God is good" is something to stand on; it is foundational to our faith. Good is not less than Excellent. The Hebrew word *good* means The Best! Even excellent is less than The Best. You can do something with excellence but not be the best. You can get a blue ribbon but not be chosen for the state fair. Only The Best is chosen for the state fair. When we say God is good, we are not saying He's okay, we are saying He is abundantly above and beyond excellent. He can take something like a stillbirth or suicide attempt and work it together for benefit. He can take an unlovable, incapable child and work in your heart to love her. He can take a "set in her ways" coworker or administrator and give them, or you, a new heart. God is so abundantly good, He can do the impossible. God's goodness is not a wimpy *okay*, it's not mediocre, it's powerful.

"As for you, you meant evil against me, but God meant it for good in order to bring about this present result." Genesis 50:20

God's goodness brings good results, beyond what we can imagine. No matter what is going on in your life, no matter how hard or harsh it is, God is still good. When we don't understand why something awful happened, we remember, God is good. By faith we cling to the knowledge that He is good, we reach out and take hold of the hem of His robe and cling to the fact that He is good. We can trust Him to work good "all the time."

Week 30 Day 2: Sick and Tired

I'm not talking about you today, I'm talking about the kids. Round about now they are getting sick and tired of each other, like siblings on a long trip to Disneyland. They have been stuck in the car with each other for days. Disneyland (summer) is looming at the end of the trip but they cannot tolerate another hour with each other. "His junk is on my desk." "Her feet are on my floor." "She follows me around and won't let me alone." "He's gross and annoying." Often a Christian School is small and the kids have been together since preschool. They are family. But they are ready for a break from each other. They have forgotten how much they really love each other.

"Then the whole congregation of the children of Israel complained against Moses and Aaron in the wilderness." Exodus 16:2 NKJV

Moses dealt with complaining too. At least you are only facing a couple months, not forty years. God answered Moses' complainers by sending manna. You could use some manna yourself. To be honest, there is not much you can do that will have a lasting effect. It's the *endure to the end* time of year. But don't give up, get out your tool bag. If you don't do something, you'll hear the chorus, "I'm not coming back to this school next year cause everybody's mean to me."

It's time to include more brain breaks and class/team building activities. Get them to have fun working together. Go outside and play some old-fashioned recess games like Pom Pom Pullaway, Red Light Green Light, or Blind Man's Bluff. Sing, dance, and be silly now and then. I know you have a lot to teach before the end of the year, but you will accomplish more with happy kids than grumpy kids.

"A merry heart does good, like medicine, But a broken spirit dries the bones." Proverbs 17:22 NKJV

Laughing together will remind them they really do love each other. And it will remind you too!

Week 30 Day 3: The Great Gap

"I SEARCHED FOR A MAN AMONG THEM WHO WOULD BUILD UP THE WALL AND STAND IN THE GAP BEFORE ME FOR THE LAND." EZEKIEL 22:30

This is the time of year the line is drawn, who is staying and who is moving on. Kids are reenrolled or not, teacher contracts are signed or not. It's hard to stand in the gap when others are not. When others are leaving, we doubt our own call to stand.

We are a family. We feel hurt when parents decide to send their kids to a different school. As teachers, we put a lifetime of love into a nine-month relationship. For the rest of our life they will be "our kids." We train ourselves to let them go, whether to the next grade or another school. We know we have to let go, but that doesn't make it easy. We give them a bushel basket of love and it feels like they reject it. We understand it has to be this way. They either move up or out and we have to let them, it's what we do. We remain, standing in the gap; the gap between our love for them and their need to spread their wings and fly.

"THERE IS A TIME FOR EVERYTHING, A SEASON FOR EVERY ACTIVITY UNDER THE HEAVENS:…A TIME TO PLANT AND A TIME TO UPROOT." ECCLESIASTES 3:1–2 NIV

During this season when we are accosted with rumblings of who is staying and who is going, who is standing and who is walking away, we listen. We stand in the gap, and we listen for the still small voice. God is looking for those who will stand and continue to build up the wall. When it seems like the wall is crumbling a bit, God calls us to be among the gap standers.

"SO TOO, AT THE PRESENT TIME THERE IS A REMNANT CHOSEN BY GRACE." ROMANS 11:5 NIV

Week 30 Day 4: Standing in the Gap

"I SEARCHED FOR A MAN AMONG THEM WHO WOULD BUILD UP THE WALL AND STAND IN THE GAP BEFORE ME FOR THE LAND." EZEKIEL 22:30

Yesterday we talked about this season of sifting where people decide whether to stay at your wonderful school or not. It's a decision you might take personally, but you should not. You are not left-over broccoli sitting in the fridge till you mold. You are not "less than" because God is calling others away. Maybe they are seed sowers who broadcast their seed widely, but you are a builder. Maybe they are evangelistic, and you are a shepherd. Take confidence and comfort in the fact God calls you to stand—in the gap.

You, along with your fellow gap-standers, are filling a space; a space that would be empty without you. Being a bit older, I have lost several molars on both sides of my mouth. Believe me when I say gaps are problematic. God's plans for you and your school run much better when you fill a gap.

"SO TOO, AT THE PRESENT TIME THERE IS A REMNANT CHOSEN BY GRACE." ROMANS 11:5 NIV

A remnant might sound a lot like left-over broccoli—an undesirable item, but it's not. It's something that remains, a remainder. We all know how problems are often incorrect without a remainder! A remnant is important. Just the other day I pulled out a quilt I had started a couple years ago and decided to finish it. All it needed was the border. Do you think I could find any remnants of the cloth so I could finish it up? No. Evidently, on a cleaning binge, I threw out all those remnants.

When others walk away, we are remnants faithfully standing in the gap, building up our students and our school. We are chosen by grace to be remnants, like Paul. Gap-standing remnants like Ezra and Nehemiah. Chosen by grace to do what we do, to build up, to stand, to remain.

"BUT YOU ARE A CHOSEN PEOPLE, A ROYAL PRIESTHOOD, A HOLY NATION, GOD'S SPECIAL POSSESSION." 1 PETER 2:9A NIV

Chosen, not left behind.

Week 30 Day 5: Monitor and Adjust

You do this all day long. 1. You introduce a new concept. 2. The kiddos don't understand. 3. You notice because you are always watching for understanding. 4. You adjust. You throw out your original plan and go at it from a different angle. You don't even think about it. It's like driving home from school, you just automatically go, checking your mirrors, flipping the turn signal, applying the brakes. You go into driving mode. Just as you have a driving mode, you also have a teacher mode. Teaching is in your blood, so you automatically monitor and adjust.

"BUT THE PEOPLE REFUSED TO LISTEN TO SAMUEL. 'NO!' THEY SAID. 'WE WANT A KING OVER US.'" 1 SAMUEL 8:19 NIV

God had plans. He intended to be a king to His people. They didn't care for God's plan so He monitored and adjusted, He gave them a king. Just as He knew it would, things went awry with Saul so once again God monitored and adjusted–He anointed David.

God is a monitoring and adjusting God. When we mess up His plan for our lives, He monitors and adjusts. He never says, "They messed up so bad, I'm throwing this objective out."

"GOD'S LAW WAS GIVEN SO THAT ALL PEOPLE COULD SEE HOW SINFUL THEY WERE, BUT AS PEOPLE SINNED MORE AND MORE, GOD'S WONDERFUL GRACE BECAME MORE ABUNDANT." ROMANS 5:20 NLT

We mess up. Sometimes emotions run high in class and we say the wrong thing or in speaking with a parent, we aren't as tactful as we should be. We wish there was a delete button but there isn't. However, there is grace. We mess up, God sees and pours out His grace with forgiveness and a back-up plan. Thank heavens, He is never short of inspiration!

God has plans for us, objectives, and He will monitor and adjust until the objectives are met. Just like you do for your kiddos because you love them.

Week 31

Week 31 Day 1: Standardized Testing

You've never prayed so hard over attendance or fretted more over tardies than this week. This week is either a gold star or a red one on your *ability* chart. Fair or not, we take those test scores personal. Some years we have an exceptional class and their test scores soar. We proudly wear our gold star, secretly knowing it had nothing to do with any skill on our part. Other years we have a sweet class of plunkers. We work our tails off differentiating, tutoring one on one, games, study guides, pulling all the tricks out of our bag. Their scores reflect their ability. We wear our red star knowing it could have been worse. It's sad because without all the extra prayer and effort on our part, those scores *would* have been much worse. Our red star should be accompanied by pats on the back and high fives but instead, after all our work, after all the kid's work, we're left feeling embarrassed.

"JOSEPH, TO WHOM SHE WAS ENGAGED, WAS A RIGHTEOUS MAN AND DID NOT WANT TO DISGRACE HER PUBLICLY, SO HE DECIDED TO BREAK THE ENGAGEMENT QUIETLY." MATTHEW 1:19 NLT

Joseph would understand our embarrassment. He was doing everything right: walking uprightly before God, treating Mary with respect, and working hard. Then something happened totally out of his control. He's embarrassed. He loves Mary, has sacrificed for her, but now, the apple of his eye has left him embarrassed.

It's not fair that test scores should reflect our ability. We are not working with machines that can be oiled to work better. We are working with little people who are wonderfully and fearfully and *differently* made. It's not fair that you should be embarrassed for a job well done. It's not fair that the essential oils you diffused or the peppermints you provided didn't work a miracle in the kiddo who doesn't know a fraction from a chemical reaction. It wasn't fair that Mary and Joseph had to face their friends and family who could count months. But they did, knowing in their hearts they were pure. Sometimes knowing you did your best has to be enough. Sometimes knowing God gives you the gold star has to be enough.

Week 31 Day 2: Standardized Testing Part 2

In spite of the pressure to have my kids excel, I love testing week. I didn't love it as much when I taught second grade and had to read nearly everything to them. Dry throat, cough, cough. But in fourth grade I thoroughly enjoy testing.

"Then he said to me, 'Write, 'Blessed are those who are invited to the marriage supper of the Lamb.'" Revelation 19:9

At my school we ask parents to send in special healthy snacks for the class during testing week. Each day one family sends in juice boxes and another sends in food. After a couple hours of testing we set out the marriage supper of the Lamb, a buffet. It has become a bit of a competition, which kid's family brings in the best snack. One brings in cheese sticks and strawberries, another brings in strawberry shortcake and whipped cream! Both snacks are fruit and dairy, but the interpretation of *healthy snack* becomes somewhat blurred. Veggie plates and fruit plates and cheese plates! As my teacher daughter says, "It's like Templeton at the fair," in Charlotte's Web. And, as if that weren't enough, it's a week of no lesson plans and no papers to grade. A counter full of yummy snacks and an empty plan book. Sometimes a parent even brings in a gourmet tea or coffee for a hard-working teacher! Testing week is a good example of God's love.

"But you, O Lord, are a God merciful and gracious, Slow to anger and abundant in lovingkindness and truth." Psalm 86:15

God's love is abundant. Way more abundant than a smorgasbord of snacks! His love and blessing have no sorrow added. One testing day, as my daughter was contemplating a stealthy stroll to the snack counter, a student got up to search for the best carrots in the bowl. As she picked her way through the carrots, my daughter remembered noticing her picking through something else just a few moments earlier—her nose. Suddenly, the smorgasbord did not seem appealing! There was sorrow added! But God's love is pure and good and kind, and lavished upon us.

No sorrow added.

Week 31 Day 3:
Present

When I was a kid in school, every day the teacher would call roll and if I was there, I would answer, "Present."

"GOD IS OUR REFUGE AND STRENGTH, A VERY PRESENT HELP IN TROUBLE." PSALM 46:1

The Hebrew word *present* means: ready, to serve, be enough, take hold, and deliver. When I said, "Present," it meant I was there, that's all. When God says, "Present," it's so much more. But that's not all; He isn't just present in all those ways, He's *very* present, vehemently, wholly, diligently, exceedingly present!

As you and your kiddos knuckle down for state testing, you need to understand this. God is your vehemently sufficient help. He can help your kids shine like you can't imagine. They have supernatural help to tap into, and so do you. Both you and the kids need to be praying your way through these tests. This very present Help can enable them to understand things they wouldn't ordinarily understand. We can pray that God will "give you spiritual wisdom and insight so that you might grow in your knowledge of God" (Ephesians 1:17 NLT). Grow in the knowledge of the One Who created all things. That's pretty good help and that help is very present!

When I was taking the big test to get my Arizona teaching certificate, I cheated. The math section was my biggest worry. There was one question that I just couldn't understand. I read it and read it but had no idea how to work it. I stopped and prayed and read the question again. Suddenly the lightbulb came on! Suddenly I understood what the question was asking, and I understood how to answer it! My Help was very present. I ended up getting 100% on the math section! It was truly a miracle.

As you hover over your little test takers, praying they will shine, your very present Help is hovering too, enlightening their understanding, giving them the mind of Christ, and dispensing peace. Maybe you should grab a little of that peace for yourself.

Week 31 Day 4: Weeds

My yard is full of weeds—I don't do yard work during the school year. Today as I looked out at the weeds towering over my grass, it reminded me of my mind. I've been really working to resist critical thinking, you know, the bad kind where you think critical thoughts about others. Critical judging thoughts are weeds that ruin the lovely landscape of my mind. They are polluters. I've been pulling them out as soon as they pop up and I'm actually feeling pretty good about it.

"BUT WHILE EVERYONE WAS SLEEPING, HIS ENEMY CAME AND SOWED WEEDS AMONG THE WHEAT, AND WENT AWAY." MATTHEW 13:25 NIV

My mind—like my yard—doesn't just have one kind of weed. While I've been pulling out the cattails of criticism, the pokeweeds of a poverty mentality are taking over! I didn't even realize it. Suddenly the lawn of my mind is covered with a poverty attitude. It makes sense though. Teachers don't make big salaries and they spend a lot of what they make on their students and classroom. We are easy prey to a poverty spirit. We worry about how we'll pay for dental visits and new tires. We imagine conversations with the vet, trying to convince her to have mercy on our pet, cheaply. Our mind goes round and round imagining conversations where we explain to people why we can't afford this or that. Such thought patterns are the fiery darts of a spirit of poverty.

"AND MY GOD WILL MEET ALL YOUR NEEDS ACCORDING TO THE RICHES OF HIS GLORY IN CHRIST JESUS." PHILIPPIANS 4:19 NIV

Instead of imagining scenarios where God fails to meet our needs we should be thinking about the truth. God is well able to meet our needs and He promises to do it. Poverty thoughts are weeds we need to pull up and burn. Instead of trying to imagine who might loan us money to get through to payday, instead of applying for credit cards, we need to cast our cares where they belong, at the feet of Jesus. Trying to fix things on our own will end up failing and possibly taking us into debt instead of out. The Lord wants to supply our needs. He wants us to trust Him to take good care of us. We must pull out the weeds of doubt.

"WE DEMOLISH ARGUMENTS AND EVERY PRETENSION THAT SETS ITSELF UP AGAINST THE KNOWLEDGE OF GOD, AND WE TAKE CAPTIVE EVERY THOUGHT TO MAKE IT OBEDIENT TO CHRIST." 2 CORINTHIANS 10:5 NIV

Week 31 Day 5: Aggressive

Be aggressive, be be aggressive! Can you hear the cheer in your head? I heard something like this from the Lord the other night. The times we live in, the times we teach in, require spiritual aggression. This is not a time to be spiritually lazy. Just as we plan for fire and lock down drills, so also, we must be alert and aggressive spiritually.

A few months ago, I went riding with my grandson who was practicing for his driver's license. As a new driver, he was very alert. Everything he did was intentional. He was definitely *not* on autopilot. There was a time I used to drive thirty miles to school each day. I can remember suddenly looking around and wondering where I was. I drove the road so often it was automatic, I could do it passively. We can become passive in our Christianity. Pray, read the Bible, go to church–it can be done automatically. That is spiritual laziness. The Lord wants us to be spiritually aggressive.

We often admire people who can do things effortlessly. For some kids, math or reading is effortless. Christianity should *not* be effortless.

"AS THE DEER LONGS FOR STREAMS OF WATER, SO I LONG FOR YOU, O GOD." PSALM 42:1 NLT

The word aggressive means lively, with an appetite, fresh, springing. God wants us to long, to seek, and hunger for Him. None of those words are passive. They all have an edge of aggression.

Think of the very capable kiddo who never does their homework and always does the least possible to get by. They are academically passive. Don't you wish they'd wake up, push in, and be hungry to learn? The Lord desires the same from us.

"AND YOU MUST LOVE THE LORD YOUR GOD WITH ALL YOUR HEART, ALL YOUR SOUL, ALL YOUR MIND, AND ALL YOUR STRENGTH." MARK 12:30 NLT

Nothing is passive about how God wants to be loved. No autopilot Christianity, no spiritual laziness, but love with all your being.

Week 32

 # Week 32 Day 1: Drained

"AND SUDDENLY, A WOMAN WHO HAD A FLOW OF BLOOD FOR TWELVE YEARS CAME FROM BEHIND AND TOUCHED THE HEM OF HIS GARMENT." MATTHEW 9:20 NKJV

It hasn't been twelve years, but you feel like you've been losing your life's blood for a while now. Day after day you pour out your life. Maybe this class is especially hard or maybe there are difficulties at home, but whatever it is, you feel depleted. Only a few more weeks of school but like the woman in our verse, you wonder if you'll make it. You don't necessarily dread going to school, you just feel drained of what it takes to face a school day. Do you have the strength, love, and enthusiasm you need to muster in order to make it through another week? Muster? Do you even have anything that can be assembled to muster? After eight months you are drained.

This woman in our verse touched the lowest and least part of Jesus. She was walking in the shadow of death and she reached out to the very least thing that was connected to Jesus. But even so, she was healed. She reached out for a scrap and received almighty power. I often imagine myself grabbing hold of Jesus' hem and hanging on for dear life, but this is not what she did; she only touched His hem. I wonder if she even needed to touch it. I wonder if the act of reaching out to Him was enough, like putting a magnet on the fridge, as you get close the magnet pulls itself to the metal. Was it her act of reaching that pulled the power to herself?

"IN YOUR PRESENCE IS FULLNESS OF JOY." PSALM 16:11B

The woman reached out, came in contact with Jesus' presence, and was healed. It's His presence we need. We ask for our daily bread and it's in His presence we will find it. Life is in His presence. All that we need in order to finish the year strong is found in God's presence.

Reach for it.

Week 32 Day 2: Breeds

"AS THE BOYS GREW UP, ESAU BECAME A SKILLFUL HUNTER. HE WAS AN OUTDOORSMAN, BUT JACOB HAD A QUIET TEMPERAMENT, PREFERRING TO STAY AT HOME." GENESIS 25: 27 NLT

I've had two dogs of different breeds. My current dog is Sam Schnauzer. Schnauzers are bred to be ratters. He's an alarm going off when anyone comes near the house. He's alert, energetic, and independent.

My previous dog was Pug Boat Willie. Pugs are bred to be buddies. They live and breathe to be near you. While Sam lays nearby, Willie was *on* me. He would cry and howl if left alone. Sam sleeps when I'm gone, he considers it being off duty. Like Esau and Jacob, these two breeds couldn't be more different. But I love them both dearly.

What breeds do you have in your class this year? The administrative (bossy) assistant teacher, a sort of collie kiddo? Or a beagle, always nose to the ground, hunting for trouble? The glamor girl poodles? A mutt? The greyhound, always racing? A freckle-faced dalmatian? A hyper yorkie? Each breed, so different, all thrown together in your classroom. What a mix! But you love them all.

You can't teach an old dog new tricks and you can't teach different breeds using the same tricks. To train Willie I used love and cuddles as a reward. Sam could care less for cuddles, he needs treats.

Similarly, our kiddos are different breeds, so we differentiate. We find what works for each one because we want to train them well. We want to teach to their bent, their breed.

"I WILL GIVE THANKS TO YOU, FOR I AM FEARFULLY AND WONDERFULLY MADE." PSALM 139:14A

Fearfully, wonderfully, *and differently* made. And wouldn't life be boring if they were all the same breed?

Delightfully different.

Week 32 Day 3: The Brick Wall

Here you are, smack up against a brick wall. Maybe it's the administration or a parent or a kid or maybe it's a situation at home, but whatever it is, you are up against it and no progress can be made until it's gone.

"NOW THE GATES OF JERICHO WERE SECURELY BARRED BECAUSE OF THE ISRAELITES." JOSHUA 6:1A NIV

Joshua faced the brick wall of Jericho. He couldn't bring it down. He couldn't reason it down— you can't reason with a brick wall. He couldn't push it down, any idea he thought of would be ineffective. It was an impossible situation and there was nothing Joshua could do to change it; nothing but obey God. Brick walls take supernatural help.

Rahab faced the wall too. Trapped in the prison of a lifestyle she had either foolishly chosen or was forced into. She was labeled: Rahab the harlot. That's all she could ever be behind that brick wall. The wall held her in an impossible situation. Obediently she hung a red rope out her window, a gesture of reaching for a God she didn't really know.

Joshua was a bold man of God. He'd had experience with God's supernatural help, so he stepped out confidently, following God's directions, entrusting that brick wall of impossibility to God.

Rahab didn't have experience with God, but she had heard about Him and something in her lifted, something like hope, so she threw out her life line. Imagine how she must have felt as she watched the Army of Israel march confidently around her brick wall day after day. Hope grew. She watched as God dealt with her brick wall. She knew only supernatural help could bring it down.

"WHEN THE TRUMPETS SOUNDED, THE ARMY SHOUTED ... THE WALL COLLAPSED." JOSHUA 6:20A NIV

No catapults, no explosives, no strength of man brought down the brick wall of Joshua and Rahab. They obeyed and God brought it down. He will do the same for your brick wall.

Throw out that red rope.

Week 32 Day 4: Show and Teach

"SHOW ME YOUR WAYS, LORD, TEACH ME YOUR PATHS." PSALM 25:4 NIV

I have a love/hate relationship with show and tell. When you run out of plans for the day, show and tell is a great filler. It's also a time waster if it doesn't have some boundaries. In first grade one year a little boy brought his soccer ball every single show and tell. It showed us his ways and taught us his paths. Obviously, soccer was important to him. Either that or he just kept it in his backpack and pulled it out every Friday.

David asks God for show and tell. He wants to know God's ways: mode of action, conversation, and direction. And he wants to know His paths, His familiar route. David doesn't want to see a soccer ball every week. He wants to know God intimately, His character, how He thinks, the way He does things, the depths of Him. Both "show" and "path" mean instruct, among other things. David wants instruction. Not the stand and lecture kind of instruction but the down and dirty: lead, demonstrate, hands on, panning for gold, full engagement kind. All the things we teachers do every day.

David wanted what we hope our kids will want. That they won't be satisfied with merely a soccer ball, the most shallow relationship with God, but will hunger for a show and teach intimate growing knowing relationship with God.

"WE CONTINUALLY ASK GOD TO FILL YOU WITH THE KNOWLEDGE OF HIS WILL.... SO THAT YOU MAY LIVE A LIFE WORTHY OF THE LORD ... GROWING IN THE KNOWLEDGE OF GOD." COLOSSIANS 9–10 NIV

Grow and know.

Week 32 Day 5: Grace

You move through your day. You draw them in with a great anticipatory set during Bible, lots of active participation in Math, a cooperative learning structure for Language, you do what you do. Grab Marco a tissue, take a moment for a little one-on-one with Noelle, share a private joke, pat a little back, sneak a snack to a rumbly tummy. These are the things you do every day, the things you've been doing for these kiddos eight months now.

It's automatic. You don't think about it, it's who you are; but you are changing lives. You are making your kiddos love school and learning, and you're sending them the message that they are valuable and loveable.

"AND GOD'S GRACE WAS SO POWERFULLY AT WORK IN THEM ALL."
ACTS 4:33B NIV

You are a vessel of grace. Grace is powerfully at work in your students and you are the instrument through which it flows. And that little guy, feet on the seat of his chair, crouching like a frog ready to spring, he requires a little more grace than some of the others.

The year is nearly over. You are bone tired. Grace is there for you too. Grace will keep you going even as it keeps pouring out of you.

"PROPHESY OVER THESE BONES AND SAY TO THEM, 'O DRY BONES, HEAR THE WORD OF THE LORD.'" EZEKIEL 37:4B

God's grace is sufficient. Hang in there. Your dry bones will live!

Week 33

Week 33 Day 1: Behinder

The hurrier I go, the behinder I get could be your motto for the rest of the year. You work so hard to get everything done that needs to be done and it seems like you are just falling farther behind. There are so many loose ends! You still have content you want to teach and grades you need to gather. There are lots of extra activities this time of year that encroach on your class time as well as your personal time. You wonder how you will manage it all.

"AND IT CAME TO PASS, AS HE SOWED, SOME FELL BY THE WAYSIDE."
MARK 4:4A KJV

This time of year *came to pass*. It will pass and you cannot slow it down. You are on a runaway sled headed down a slippery slope. It's not a bad thing, everyone is ready for the year to end. Everyone's eyes are fixed on the finish line. You still have a bag full of batons you want to pass off to your fellow little runners, but you don't have the distance to do it. Like our verse says, some must fall to the wayside. You might as well draw a line in the sand and face the fact that not everything will get done. You are just stressing yourself out thinking about it.

"BUT THERE THEY ARE, OVERWHELMED WITH DREAD, WHERE THERE WAS NOTHING TO DREAD." PSALM 53:5A NIV

Take a deep breath and let it go. Stop trying to be Martha and get a million things done, things the kids are not able to absorb at this late date. Be Mary. Sit at Jesus' feet and pour out your perfume. Seed will fall to the wayside. Let it go. Do what you can and don't stress about the rest. Enjoy these last weeks with your kiddos. Let them enjoy it too. End well. "Well" does not equal the amount of work accomplished. It's the flavor you leave with your kiddos. What taste will you leave in their mouths when the year is over? The bitter taste of drudgery, getting work done? Or the sweet taste of shared laughter and tears, experiences and happy memories? Let what is bitter fall to the wayside and let the perfume fill your room.

Week 33 Day 2: Bless You

"Bless your little heart." Say it with a southern accent. My daughter lives in Arkansas and she tells me "Bless your little heart," isn't always a blessing in the south. Sometimes they say it in place of the insult they're actually thinking. For example, when Leroy says he didn't do his history study guide because he had a baseball game, you could say, "Well, bless your little heart." What you're really thinking is, "There's another strike out in the grade book, Babe Ruth!"

"Esau said to his father, 'Do you have only one blessing, my father? Bless me, even me also, O my father.' So Esau lifted his voice and wept." Genesis 27:38

Esau knew how powerful a blessing is. He came to the knowledge a little late, but he realized it just the same, and begged for it. You know the power in it too. Remember those little notes? "You are the best teacher." "I love you Mrs. Jones." "You are my favorite teacher." Don't they just bless your little heart? Well, it's the time of the year to bless your kiddo's little hearts back and not in a southern way, in a sincere way. From here on out the year is going to get crazy and if you aren't careful it will get away from you before you bless their little hearts. Find some time to jot a little note of blessing or at least to speak it to every student.

"How blessed is the one whom You choose and bring near to You To dwell in Your courts. We will be satisfied with the goodness of Your house, Your holy temple." Psalm 65:4

What a blessing we have as teachers, chosen to be brought near to impact the hearts of children for Christ. Let's pass the blessing forward. Bless their little hearts—and mean it.

Week 33 Day 3: Prison

There are times we feel like our life is a prison. It might be school, grief, finances, a situation at home, unfulfilled dreams, or a million other things, things we can't control or break free of.

"AFTER BEING SEVERELY FLOGGED, THEY WERE THROWN INTO PRISON." ACTS 16:23A NIV

Can you relate to Paul and Silas? There were many times during my husband's battle with dementia, I could. I was teaching full time and going home to *heaven knows what*. I felt flogged and thrown in prison. That is no way to live life. When we feel imprisoned in our own lives, we need to seek a way to happiness in the midst of our prison.

"ABOUT MIDNIGHT PAUL AND SILAS WERE PRAYING AND SINGING HYMNS TO GOD." ACTS 16:25A NIV

We must find a way to sing in prison. How? We make time to get our focus off the prison and on the hills where our help comes from. We cannot just sit, flogged, on a prison bench, hating our life. We will become bitter and fruitless if we do. Our kiddos will suffer, and we will suffer. The truth is, God has plans for us. This prison is a season. God wouldn't allow it if there weren't benefit. Every season has its difficulties and joys. In the hard winter there is sledding. In the dry summer there is swimming. In our prison it's all about attitude. We can rot in the stocks or sing in the cell. But rotting will not swing open any doors.

"AT ONCE ALL THE PRISON DOORS FLEW OPEN, AND EVERYONE'S CHAINS CAME LOOSE." ACTS 16:26B NIV

Your chains *will* come loose. Your prison doors *will* open. You might as well sing in the meantime.

Week 33 Day 4: Daily

Daily Oral Language, daily math drill, lunch count, pledges. These are habits you do on a daily basis. God has daily tasks too.

"Blessed be the Lord, who daily bears our burden." Psalm 68:19a

Instead of Daily Oral Language, God daily bears our burdens.

You would think our burden would be lighter here at the end of the year, but it's not. We have so many things we still need to do. You would think by now the kiddos would be easier to work with because we know each other so well, but that's not the case. Our kiddos have become monkeys. So there's the burden of trying to accomplish much with a bunch of monkeys. It's good to know each new day our burdens are carried by our good good God.

"Give us this day our daily bread." Matthew 6:11

Maybe I'm wrong, but I always interpret *our bread* as everything we need. It's so comforting that daily God meets our needs. Whether it's energy, wisdom, or an actual loaf of bread, He daily provides.

"Great is his faithfulness; his mercies begin afresh each morning." Lamentations 3:23 NLT

This is my favorite: daily mercy each morning. No matter what went on yesterday, no matter what the burdens, today I have fresh new mercies. Daily. Faithfully. Never failing.

Week 33 Day 5: New Song

"HE PUT A NEW SONG IN MY MOUTH, A SONG OF PRAISE TO OUR GOD."
PSALM 40:3A

You cross another day off the year-end calendar. Three weeks to go. Isn't it a little late in the year for a new song? Your goal is just to survive to the end of the year, you don't have the energy for anything new, let alone a new song. You are in "Please don't add one more thing to my overloaded plate" mode. If anyone asks you to do something, the answer is, no. It's automatic, you don't even have to think about it. "No, No, No, don't even ask!"

But wait a minute. This new song isn't something we have to do, it's something given to us, a gift. God will put it in our mouth! Oh, and look again! It's not something He's going to give us later, like when school is out; He already did it, He put a new song in our mouth. It's already there. Remember the scene in Christmas Vacation where Clark Griswold goes to the attic to hide gifts and finds old gifts hidden there he'd forgotten about? He already had gifts, wrapped and everything. All he'd have to do was pull down the attic stairs and get them.

It's the same for us, all we have to do is reach for that new song. It's waiting. A fresh mindset, crisp inspiration, renewed energy. We'll find it all in His Presence.

Week 34

Week 34 Day 1: Two More

Oh, my goodness! After today there are only two more Mondays in this year! Only two more Mondays of getting up early and heading to school to make a fresh week. Fresh week? It's getting hard to make anything fresh these days. Both you and the kids are ready to be done. Getting and keeping their attention takes an act of God. Our little community has a big fair this time of year and that always stirs up the year-end crazies. But even without a fair there is rain, wind, full moons, donuts for breakfast, allergies, and even silly bees stumbling into the classroom to stir things up. It doesn't take much for us to lose it.

While there are technically three weeks of school, there are only two more weeks of teaching and grading! The tricky part is, there are zero weeks of learning left. So, while we are teaching and grading, the kids are no longer sponges absorbing our teaching. They are rocks, meteors spinning through outer space, oblivious to any teaching taking place. And you? You are starting a fifteen-day Jericho march. You will march through these days with determination. You will keep moving forward hoping your troops will follow, even though they have forgotten how to march in a line. Good grief.

"THE ARMED GUARD MARCHED AHEAD OF THE PRIESTS WHO BLEW THE TRUMPETS, AND THE REAR GUARD FOLLOWED THE ARK. ALL THIS TIME THE TRUMPETS WERE SOUNDING." JOSHUA 6:9 NIV

You are the armed guard marching ahead of your trumpeteers and you could sure use a rear guard!

"DO NOT RAISE YOUR VOICES, DO NOT SAY A WORD UNTIL THE DAY I TELL YOU TO SHOUT." JOSHUA 6:10 NIV

This week you will attempt to keep an orderly calm classroom. This is probably the last week you can get away with any semblance of order. You are too tired to be Joshua with his millions of stiff-necked rebels, but you do it anyway. You take a deep breath, say a prayer, and clamp down the lid for a week of attempted sanity. You can do it. You are a trained professional. You have sufficient grace and daily mercy to count on. Reach up and pull down that anointing, the mantle of the double portion.

You can do it!

 # Week 34 Day 2: His Will

"Your kingdom come. Your will be done, On earth as it is in heaven." Matthew 6:10

The Lord's Prayer. We teach it to our kids. We say it rotely with little thought to what it means. But it is Jesus' powerful example of prayer and it deserves more than a recitation.

Back before cell phones were common, my family made several treks to Disneyland. I'd get a map at the gate and live by it. We didn't know our way around very well back then so after every ride I'd pull the map out of my pocket to figure out where to go next. By the end of the trip my map was a limp rag. I think the Lord intends His prayer to be like my Disneyland map, something used and used, and used again. Not something framed and hung on the wall, a pleasant memory, but something crucial to getting through our day.

I pull the Lord's Prayer out of my pocket nearly every day and it shows me the way to pray. The other day a question came to mind: Would God ever say no to doing His will? If I pray, "Lord, work your will in my classroom," will He respond negatively? Will He say, "No, I'm not going to do My will?" Of course not. If we ask for His will, that's exactly what He'll do. What a powerful thing, to partner with God, ask His will and watch Him manifest it.

So, if I pray, "Lord please work Your will in every student who goes through my classroom." Will He do it? I have to believe He will.

"If you ask Me anything in My name, I will do it." John 14:14

Week 34 Day 3: To Be Continued

Two and a half weeks of school left, and Joey still can't remember his multiplication facts. Ugh! You've tried everything you know to do, and you've failed. You want so badly for every one of your kiddos to succeed. But have you really failed? You began a good work in Joey, you did everything you could think of to help him. That is not failure. Now you trust God to continue the work.

"AND I AM CERTAIN THAT GOD, WHO BEGAN THE GOOD WORK WITHIN YOU, WILL CONTINUE HIS WORK UNTIL IT IS FINALLY FINISHED ON THE DAY WHEN CHRIST JESUS RETURNS." PHILIPPIANS 1:6 NLT

I confess, I didn't understand working with fractions until I had to teach them. I went through grade school, high school, and college just guessing on fraction problems. Teacher after teacher tried to explain it to me, they did their best, they began a good work, but I didn't understand until years later. When I needed to understand, God picked up the work my teachers began, and He continued it in me until I got it.

It's hard to send a kiddo off without a skill you feel responsible for. Will the next teacher be able to help him? There is only so much you can do. You begin a work and pass it on to someone else. Each teacher does their best, it's all God expects of you.

You haven't failed, you've began a good work. The Lord will be faithful to complete it.

 # Week 34 Day 4: Still

"Be still, and know that I am God." Psalm 46:10a ESV

You walk around your quiet classroom. The only sounds are pages turning and pencils scratching. It's a precious and rare moment. No, it's not standardized testing; you are teaching your students to be still with God.

The word *still* in Psalm 46 means: to slacken, cease, to draw toward, to stay. It also seems to indicate a vulnerability. We are to cease our busy pace of learning and teaching, slow things down, draw near to God, and stay there a bit in honest vulnerability.

Many times I have my kiddos get under their desks with their Bible and journal to get a nugget from God. I'm teaching them to be still and know Him. Afterward I have them share a verse or a word in order to build their confidence. I'm giving them a gift much greater than chocolate.

"He leads me beside still waters." Psalm 23:2b ESV

In our clamorous chaotic culture, being still doesn't come naturally. It's crucial that we teach it. It's in the stillness we feel God's presence and hear His voice. Psalm 46 says, in the stillness we come to know God.

Before you send this lively little brood off for the summer, make some time to remind them how to be still and hear God. In a quiet cave a still small voice came to Elijah and gave him direction to move forward. Your kiddos need to hear it too.

Week 34 Day 5: Flourish

"Those that be planted in the house of the Lord shall flourish in the courts of God." Psalm 92:13 KJV

Flourish means to break forth as a bud, to bloom, and to spread the wings and fly. It's hard to think of flourishing right now. Two weeks down the road it will be easy but now, not so much. You are facing two weeks of very excited kiddos and your energy level is as low as your plate is piled high. You don't have the time or strength to spread your wings and fly.

Does it really take effort to flourish? Psalm 92:12 says the righteous man will flourish. Jesus is our righteousness so He's the one Who put forth the effort for us to flourish. Verse thirteen says we who are planted will flourish and according to Isaiah, we are a planting of the Lord. So, it sounds like we can flourish even in adversity.

I have seen a crocus bloom in the snow, and I've seen a cardinal fly in a hundred fifteen-degree temperatures. Both were flourishing in difficult circumstances. In fact, isn't it often adversity that brings us the most growth? Here at the end of the year we can allow ourselves to be beat down by overwhelming situations or we can draw near to the One Who planted us and we can flourish.

"I have set before you life and death, blessing and cursing: therefore choose life." Deuteronomy 30:19b KJV

Let's choose life. Flourish.

Week 35

Week 35 Day 1: Swine Show

Have you ever seen a 4-H or FFA swine show? I saw my first one this year and let me tell you, it's not at all what I expected! They bring thirty kids and their pigs into an arena. The pigs don't wear halters, so the kids coax their pig back and forth in front of the judge by gently using a little whip on them. All the time the kids are guiding their pig they have to maintain intense eye contact with the judge. Sometimes two pigs would get into a fight and men with big boards would come out and slide the boards between the bickering pigs. Some pigs would get fed up with being guided back and forth and would just start squealing non-stop, others would just take off running, leaving their kid behind. It reminded me of the last weeks of school. We are keeping constant eye contact with the last day of school while trying to corral a bunch of loose piglets and we do it without whips or guys and big boards! All the while we are trying to TEACH them something! I think we can appreciate what Moses went through, herding his millions around the wilderness.

"I HAVE SEEN THESE PEOPLE," THE LORD SAID TO MOSES, "AND THEY ARE A STIFF-NECKED PEOPLE." EXODUS 32:9 NIV

How do we keep teaching when the kids have checked out? Well, we just do. We keep our energy up when we have none. Caffeine helps. We flail our arms and do a little dance, we get out the manipulatives, we turn everything we possibly can into a game. We use every trick we have. We don't give up, we chase them around the arena if necessary. And when they start squealing non-stop, we calm them down. How? With a soft voice and a bag of candy, a promise of extra recess, letting them sit on their desk or on the floor, anything that will reel them back in for another day. Another day closer to the last day.

Week 35 Day 2: Clean

"CREATE IN ME A CLEAN HEART, O GOD; AND RENEW A RIGHT SPIRIT WITHIN ME." PSALM 51:10 KJV

I wonder if there is a verse I pray more often than this? I'm pretty sure I say it daily and possibly more. The Holy Spirit is helping me overcome a tendency to be critical and judgemental, hence the frequent use of the verse.

Today, as I was brushing my teeth, it occurred to me that getting a clean heart and right spirit is a lot like keeping your teeth clean. Brushing your teeth once will not do, brushing doesn't last. Food causes plaque and bacteria to form which makes our teeth dirty and eventually diseased. We start out the day with clean teeth but the first time we eat something, bad stuff goes to work on them. It's the same with our heart. We spend time with the Lord and start our day with a clean heart. Then someone monopolizes the copy machine before school and bacteria begins to accumulate in our heart. The duty teacher forgets to show up at recess and you end up on the playground when you need to make copies. Someone uses the last of your favorite coffee creamer. That leads to plaque. Your heart is no longer clean. We take a deep breath and brush our teeth, "Lord, please make my heart clean and my spirit right."

Bad attitude? Remember to brush and floss.

Week 35 Day 3: Having Done All

"And having done all, to stand." Ephesians 6:13b NKJV

You reach a point where you have done everything you can possibly do. From this point on, it's out of your hands. All you can do is stand. The kiddo who has never asked Jesus into her heart, there's nothing more you can do but stand on the promise that He wants none to perish. The one whose parents are splitting up, you stand on the knowledge that he is precious to the Lord. The one who still can't read well, you stand knowing you did the best you could under the circumstances.

"There is therefore now no condemnation to those who are in Christ Jesus, who do not walk according to the flesh, but according to the Spirit." Romans 8:1 NKJV

Sometimes walking in the Spirit means standing. The flesh tells us you didn't do enough, you could have done more. That's a lie. You did the best you could in the circumstances because that's what you do. The flesh wants to spotlight your lacks, but the Spirit knows you. He knows all that's on your plate. He knows your skills and He prepared you for this group of kids. He had plans for you and plans for the kids and you carried out His plans. He knew what you could do in each situation and that was His plan. You didn't let that kiddo down and you accomplished what the Lord expected from you.

Standing isn't easy. When we are standing, we reflect; and when we reflect, often times that lying voice comes after us with his fiery darts of accusation. He tells us we haven't done all. He says we failed. The Spirit says we did all; all He planned and expected from us.

"I planted, Apollos watered, but God gave the increase." 1 Corinthians 3:6 NKJV

You had a part to play in each kiddo's growth this year. It's like an assembly line. You added your part to the product. God is the designer, not you. You are not responsible for any more than adding in your part. You water but God is in charge of the outcome. He brings it all together in His plan.

You *have* done all, now you stand.

Week 35 Day 4: Rebels

"THEN I WILL TEACH YOUR WAYS TO REBELS, AND THEY WILL RETURN TO YOU."
PSALM 51:13 NLT

I had to giggle when I came upon this verse in the New Living Translation. There are plenty of days I felt like I was trying to teach God's ways to rebels. Perhaps even a rebel alliance! The great thing about this verse is, when we teach God's ways to rebels, they *will* return to Him.

I remember a girl many years ago who was taught God's ways, but she rebelled against them. She walked away from God and chose to go her own way. It will not surprise you that eventually she returned to God and His path. That girl was me—and possibly you also. It's a great comfort to those of us who spend our lives teaching God's ways to rebels, knowing our life work is not wasted. Our rebels will return to God just like we did.

God is faithful. He desires that none should perish. He continues the work He began in them. Like the Prodigal Son, they will come to their senses one day and head home. Home to their Savior and home to His ways. Jesus paid the price for them to come home.

"FOR GOD SO LOVED THE WORLD, THAT HE GAVE HIS ONLY BEGOTTEN SON, THAT WHOEVER BELIEVES IN HIM SHALL NOT PERISH, BUT HAVE ETERNAL LIFE."
JOHN 3:16

Week 35 Day 5: Doubting Thomas

"Unless I see in His hands the imprint of the nails, and put my finger into the place of the nails, and put my hand into His side, I will not believe." John 20:25b

Personally seeing the resurrected Jesus wasn't enough for Thomas. He wanted to see Jesus and see the nail prints and touch the nail prints. Oh, and that wasn't enough either; he also wanted to put his hand into Jesus' side. Good grief.

Do you have a Doubting Thomas on staff? In Professional Development they ask question after question, dragging the session on and on. Sometimes they are like a puppy who gets hold of something and just won't let go. This time of year, PD is especially hard because you don't want to be there. You try to have a good attitude but it's hard when you just want to tie up the loose ends of this year and move on. But your staff *Thomas* is doubting away; sometimes I think they just want to hear their own voice.

What do you do when Doubting Thomas shows up with their grocery list of questions and stall tactics?

"Do nothing from selfishness or empty conceit, but with humility of mind regard one another as more important than yourselves; do not merely look out for your own personal interests, but also for the interests of others." Philippians 2:3–4 NASB

While we'd like to quote this verse to Doubting Thomas, we can't. We can only apply it to ourselves. When we judge Thomas, we become the selfish prideful one, looking out for our own interests. Thomas is coming from a place of insecurity. Asking questions, lengthy discussions, putting his hand in nail prints, all these bring some sort of comfort to him. Our place is to be humble and kind, as we would have others do unto us.

Week 36

Week 36 Day 1: Last Days

"But mark this: There will be terrible times in the last days." 2 Timothy 3:1 NIV

I think Timothy may have been a teacher. In verses 3–5 he goes on to describe the people of the last days: disobedient, ungrateful, slanderous, without self-control, rash, and lovers of pleasure, to mention a few. You may be facing some of these people in the last days of school. Some of them might even be students!

Kidding aside, the last days are exhausting. You are trying to teach, or at least keep order, in the middle of a circus. Hopefully you have found some engaging activities that you saved for this, the longest week of school. Review games are great, but they won't keep the kiddos engaged a whole day. You are going to need either lots of short activities or more lengthy but very engaging projects. Don't plan on anything lasting as long as it normally would. You are dealing with fleas on a skillet here.

Even though this week is not the easiest, keep in mind this is your last week with these kids. Whether it's been a hard year or an easy one, by now you have grown to love them. What is it you really want to leave them with spiritually? Take some time early this week to pray for each of them. Ask the Lord to give you a word or a verse for each.

"Then they gathered around him and asked him, 'Lord, are you at this time going to restore the kingdom to Israel?'" Acts 1:6 NIV

One of the last things Jesus did before He was taken up to Heaven was spend intimate time with His followers. He let them ask questions and commissioned them to be His witnesses. Use this opportunity to let your little followers ask you some questions; share your testimony if you haven't already. Tell them what your hopes and dreams are for them, what you expect of them. Do it early in the week before they are totally distracted and before you are frazzled.

"The Lord bless you and keep you; the Lord make his face shine on you and be gracious to you; the Lord turn his face toward you and give you peace." Numbers 6:24–26 NIV

Speak a blessing over your kiddos, let them know they will always be special to you and to God.

Week 36 Day 2: Forgotten

You look up to see a kiddo standing on her desk. What? Have they forgotten everything? Have all the procedures you've instilled in them this year, none of which included standing on their desk, been forgotten?

"I, EVEN I, AM THE ONE WHO WIPES OUT YOUR TRANSGRESSIONS FOR MY OWN SAKE, AND I WILL NOT REMEMBER YOUR SINS." ISAIAH 43:25

God is not a rowdy year-end student forgetting how to behave, but He *has* forgotten something. And that something is our sin. Nothing we have done or neglected to do is in God's memory bank.

"AS FAR AS THE EAST IS FROM THE WEST, SO FAR HAS HE REMOVED OUR TRANSGRESSIONS FROM US." PSALM 103:12

Not only has God forgotten our sin, but He has also removed them from us. It's like they never even happened. Forgiveness is a wonderful and necessary thing, but God goes beyond forgiveness. As usual, He does exceedingly abundantly more than we could imagine: He forgets and removes our sin.

Here at the end of the year we are run ragged: grading, report cards, awards, keeping the kids engaged, taking all the evidence off the walls that we've been in this room all year, cleaning, sorting, putting everything in order. We are weary and that makes us easy prey for condemnation. Don't listen to the voice of the accuser, listen to the One who forgives, forgets, and removes. None of your lacks or shortcomings are remembered. God is standing on His desk cheering, "You're the best teacher ever!"

 # Week 36 Day 3: Hump Day

This is your last hump day for the year! Take a moment to breathe. Depending on how your school handles the last days, this may be the last full day you have to keep your kiddos focused. It may also be the last day you teach Bible.

"YOU SHALL TEACH THEM (GOD'S WORDS) DILIGENTLY TO YOUR SONS AND SHALL TALK OF THEM WHEN YOU SIT IN YOUR HOUSE AND WHEN YOU WALK BY THE WAY AND WHEN YOU LIE DOWN AND WHEN YOU RISE UP."
DEUTERONOMY 6:7

Resist the temptation to show a Bible video. Make the most of this Bible time, make it memorable.

As for the rest of the day, if you haven't already, let the kids help you take down things that need to be off the walls. I used to feel like I had to leave everything up to the very last day of school. It would take me a week or more (because I piddled around) to finish my room for the summer. I got over that. Don't waste any more of your summer than necessary. Honestly, you will be back in your room weeks before school starts next year so give yourself a break at this end.

"MY HELP COMES FROM THE LORD, WHO MADE HEAVEN AND EARTH."
PSALM 121:2

Today your help comes from the Lord—and possibly a handful of kiddos who are anxious and happy to bless you. Let both the Lord and your kiddos bless this last hump day.

Week 36 Day 4: Almost There

You are almost there!

"AND THE LORD SHOWED HIM (MOSES) THE WHOLE LAND, FROM GILEAD AS FAR AS DAN." DEUTERONOMY 34:1b NLT

You are so near to the Promised Land of summer break, so near you can see it. Imagine how Moses felt looking on his promised land, remembering all he'd walked through. Whiny, unruly tribes, tabernacles to build, close encounters with unfriendlies. It may resemble your year. But Moses also probably remembered the manna and quail, the water from a rock, and clothes that never wore out, all God's provision through the difficulties.

As you stand on Mt. Pisgah what do you see? A beach, a house project, a garden, a road trip? Whatever your summer plans are, be sure to include something fun. Allow yourself time to refresh. When my kids were young, and money was tight we would go to Grandpa's farm for a week. Grandma had been a diner cook at one time and she fed us like kings. Maybe you don't have a farm to go to but find something you can afford that will revive your spirit. I'm sure you have plenty you want to accomplish but don't leave out time to reboot.

While you're up here on Pisgah, take a moment to remember all that God has done in the wilderness of this past school year. The little guy whose light bulb came on, the spiritual growth, the breakthroughs, the laughter, and the tears. It's been a good year and you are a good teacher.

Week 36 Day 5: Ending and Sending

"Teaching them to observe all that I commanded you; and lo, I am with you always, even to the end of the age." Matthew 28:20

It's here, the day you've looked forward to since Christmas, or maybe longer. Final report cards are done, including thoughtful comments, awards signed, library books mostly accounted for, and you sit at your desk, torn. It's such a bittersweet day. You are more than ready for summer vacation but are you really ready to say good-bye to these kiddos? Some maybe, but there are those it will be hard to let go.

I have a little gourd given to me many years ago by a boy named James. James didn't have anything, not anything. But he gave me his gourd. It meant more to me than a hundred candy packed mugs. Every year I pull out the gourd when we read about them in *Swiss Family Robinson* and I tell the kids about James.

Most of the kiddos you say good-bye to today are Jameses who touch your heart in a forever way. You will say good-bye and let them fly away to summer and another teacher because that's what you do. You're a teacher. You know your time with them is limited. You knew last fall you would have to let them go. You will paste on a smile as you dab at your eyes with a tissue, and you will let them go.

Teaching is like "catch and release" fishing. You catch your kiddos; you have the thrill of the catch, the thrill of loving them and watching them grow, then you release them and let them swim away. It's easier said than done. They have become your family. But because this is what you do, you will release this family and make room in your heart for a new family a couple months down the road. You will never forget this little school of fishies and you will never stop loving them no matter how far they swim.

Just keep swimming.

www.ingramcontent.com/pod-product-compliance
Lightning Source LLC
Chambersburg PA
CBHW050316120526
44592CB00014B/1925